DID we write

Acknowledgements

We wish to thank our Mum, Granma, Doreen, who, after initially finding the whole thing very odd, and saying 'It's very peculiar' many times in the first few months, somehow got her head around this whole crazy situation (or realised she just had to go with it, for the sake of her daughter), and has been tremendously supportive. She gets phone calls from Mia and Berwoo everyday, and her patience and understanding (like Amber's) made this much easier than it might have been, not that any of it has been at all easy.

We would like to thank the three therapists who've supported us through this *revelation*. Maggie, who listened to Berlou cry for months, while Amber had no idea what was going on, or why she was crying. Emma, who supported us until we were evidently 'out of her depth', and Simon, who's been listening to us (voluntarily), for over a year; also Andy, the mental health nurse we see regularly - we couldn't have got through this without them. Thank you.

Hot Yoga Commonside - we're all eternally grateful for them, Koreen, and now their new owner, have been amazing. HYC is the one place we can go, and be ourselves. If Amber hadn't found HYC, both the yoga and the community, we wouldn't have had that wonderful place where we can go, authentically, and 'shake the trauma out'.

The friends who have stuck by us, the ones, who in spite of this very strange situation listened to and loved us. The system friends we've made through Facebook and Instagram, especially LA/BA, the Extra System, and Claire Lefferts - thank you for always being there.

Andrew Lawes who keeps reading our nonsense and supporting us, even though we don't actually know each other, we're just fellow mental health sufferers who can't stop writing. Ashlie, for proofreading this, and Mia's original manuscript of poems, and offering advice and support to myself, Mia, and probably others.

The Instagram poetry community - without their prompts, love and support, Mia would never have written the God knows how many poems she has. And every single person that's liked or commented on the hundreds of Mia's posts - thank you all.

Ben, our husband, who has understandably, struggled to grasp what on earth happened to his wife, but, nevertheless, has financially supported us and stuck with us while we figured all this out.

And Jason, our shadow, our doggo. Who loves us, worries about us, makes us walk everyday, and constantly reminds us that life can be good. Berwoo was just here, she started to thank herself, for being wonderful. I wholeheartedly agree with the sentiment, thanks Berwoo, for both being wonderful, saving us, and formatting and publishing this (the first time, a few weeks ago with Pen/Maya), and then finding me again.

- Jessica, on behalf of everyone.

Foreword

I still can't believe this is now our life, this *revelation* has been the biggest event of my life, and all I had to do was let it happen. When I'm not here, I'm not here, but when we are consciously present it seems memories are more or less recorded for all to access, and so much is now in black and white that denial is no longer an option.

As per everything that's happened, deciding to edit and publish *The revelation* made little sense at the time but in retrospect was needed. Berwoo and Pen/Maya (fusion) decided to format and edit this to publish, we weren't sure why now, but it feels like we needed to reflect on everything that's happened, so much has been forgotten and often the general feelings are that we aren't making progress, but our alters have achieved huge healing since Isabel and I found each other two years ago.

We don't know how cathartic it will be to release this, and while much of it is incredibly personal, I still have emotional detachment from a lot, which maybe makes it easier, and I feel it's worth publishing. Mia and Jessica's book shows how complex healing is, how someone who has seemed neurotypical for nearly four decades can be hiding huge secrets even from themselves. I had no idea until two years ago, and hadn't heard of DID until Isabel, Mia and Maya had been writing the experience for months. One time about twelve years ago I lived alone and during that time became plural, but remember very little from that year and don't know how it got forgotten. There were huge clues also throughout the whole life but without knowing about DID (in spite of studying psychology and health at university, we assume now that was subconsciously looking for answers) we had no opportunity to recognise this, have a much sooner *revelation*, and heal.

I am in awe of everything that Mia, Berwoo, Berlou, and many of our other alters, have achieved these two years. Mia's capability and motivation is extraordinary and I'm only sorry I've been restricting her (or versions of her) for all these years. All Berlou wants is to use our experiences to help others - it's the only way she can reconcile with the pain she's experienced throughout this lifetime and I have total confidence in Mia and Berlou, they've been through so much and can achieve anything.

- Amber

Mia

By Amber

She was always going to do great things
I just had to find her first

Contents

We keep thinking
Like
Mia's poems

-

Maya

Her

By Miya

I'm not part of her
She's not part of me
We are both part of this
I am not her
She is not me
We are separate
It's not my fault
We have the same face

Chandelier

by Maya

She imagined
The anxiety
The past
The pain
Smashing to the ground
Breaking into a thousand pieces
Like an antique chandelier
Unbearable
But
She made something beautiful
With the pieces

Expectation

By Miya

She always knew
Something
Was wrong
The feelings
The emotions
DID
Not
Make
Sense

Divided
We r
Fragmented
We
Never came together
We never
Became
One

She fought
For years
To work out
What
Was
Wrong

She never expected
To find us

Rocks and rubbish

By unknown

How many days will we have to
Dive deep into the body and soul
Digging up the dirt and past
Sifting, sorting rocks and rubbish
Dragging it all into the light
Saying this happened to me
No one cares but I shout anyway
Show them where it hurts
Let them see why I cry
Allow the feelings to take over
Entertain them in ways they never knew
Giving them space to breathe
A platform
To shout from
Allowing them to flow through
The body and the mind
Transforming translucent
Bubbles of hate and fear
As the light intermingles
The feelings dissipate
They feel the sun and remember
They weren't always here
They don't have to stay
They can fight to stay
Argue through the day and night
Insist they are right and are the only way
They don't go easily
They put up a fight
Their darkness can creep
Taking over the site

Alters and the other people you will meet

The alters

Bold are a different version of the same alter, *(italics)* is a nickname

Amber/Mummy - same person, system host, the alter who has lived most of the life
Jessica - the writer
Mia - magic unicorn fairy
Berlou/Amber Louise/AL/Berwoo - TH (trauma holder) number one, various versions of
Isabel - protector and bitch
Caris - Isabel + Cara
Maya - the other half of Mia
Penelope - enigma, an old, non-traumatised alter
Willow - mysterious helper
Kai *(It/The Thing)* - little persecutor
Tiffany/Jade/Tiger/Stef - Protector and sexual alter
Bumblebee - Berlou's doll
Mia Berlou - Mia + Berlou
Cherry - not a TH, lives inside
Miya - Mia + Maya
Lolly/Leah/Lola - TH (loneliness)
Tilly/Thalia *(Sophie/Soph)* - TH (tiredness)
Jasmine/Jas - TH (sadness)
Anabel - TH (head injury), a split from Isabel

Abigail - TH (car crash)

Cara/Little Cara *(Gollum)* - TH and soother

Alex - TH (grief)

Amex - Amber + Alex

Moody Mia - Mia + Kali

Kali - TH teens (Jas + Soph + Lola)

Tildy - Amber's doll she had as a child

Carabel - Anabel + Little Cara

Mia Alex - Mia + Alex

Peach/Peaches/Sasha - TH

Faith - little, not much known

Astrid - little, not much known, smol

Jacob/Jake - split from Isabel

Gemma - little, unknown

Amberlou - Amber + Berlou

Amberlouis - Amber + Berlou + Caris

Ray of Sunshine *(RoS/Ray)* - TH, related to Maya

The other people

Granma/Amber's Mum/Mum - same person, Amber's Mum

Dad/Amber's Dad - Amber's Dad

Pete - Amber's brother

Nana - Amber's Grandmother

Dandan - Amber's Grandfather

Nikki - Amber's oldest friend

Koreen - yoga studio owner and confidante

Vikki/Auntie DikDik - friend and littles entertainer

The Extra System - a European DID system we became close friends with

LA/BA - another system we became friends with through Facebook

MH nurse/mental nurse - a mental health nurse we see once a month

Jason - Doggo

Ray - Dead doggo

DID?

Not a poem

By Mia

DID isn't a poem
It's not something fun
It's not a show
A display of personalities
It's a disorder
Caused by trauma

The current accepted theory
Is the theory of structural dissociation
When we are little
We have different 'states'
Altered states of consciousnesses
(Hence, alters)

When trauma happens
We build amnesiac blocks
Between the states
The alters
They develop
Not knowing each other are there

So, in our case

We lived
For 38 years
Not knowing each other were here
The memories
Were just wiped

We all
Thought we were
Amber
Couldn't understand
Why her
Emotions and thoughts
Never made much sense

This book
Is disjointed
Like us
Trying to figure out
Wtaf
Happened to this brain

Hello. My name is Jessica. I'm an alter, an identity within a Dissociative Identity Disorder system - Amber Ainsworth. This book started as a book of poetry by Mia, another alter, and then we realised some explanation might be helpful, and that as this last year has been so horrifically unbelievable, that we might as well tell that story together with Mia's poems. Seeing as she is capable of a couple of highly bizarre Facebook statuses every day, and there is poetry and writing everywhere I look, I've got a lot of material to work with. So I'm here to narrate, explain a bit of the weirder stuff, fill in some gaps, and hopefully bring everything - and everyone, this is a healing endeavour, too - together. Or, in Mia's words - 'collate and narrate, quickly'.

Jessica

By Jessica

I'm a writer
Mia was lazy
Didn't want to write
But we had to get it out
Pour the feelings
Into the paper
She said
I need a writer!
I appeared
I wrote
I journaled
Could access thoughts and memories
I started writing a children's book
It was abandoned
Some time ago
Recently
She thought it would be fun
If she could write herself
She asked if I would fuse with her
I said no
It happened anyway
It was only after
Mia completed a first draft of this book
In under two weeks
That Amber
Realised I was with her
We separated again
I can now narrate
She's unique in her style
So, I'll try to intertwine

The neverending poems
Pouring from Mia, et al.
With some explanation
And our story
I hope you enjoy the ride
More than we did

Mia would like to say a few words too (she usually wants to).

Hewwo it Mia. So dis was my book first, and I am still hopefully gonna make my book of poetry bc I'm really proud off that. Jessica doing good work and we r healing as she doing dis but it also a bit poopy and a bit annoying. Even tho it my fault and I asked her to narrate haha. Anyway, it also because of my sister Berlou (we often just call each other sisters, it nice) that we write dis book. She really wants to help people and maybe us telling our story can help other people heal bc omg this is hard and scary at times. We hope it might be interesting enuff that people wiffout DID might want to read it too, and that good bc then we r raising awareness. That important. Fanx for reading, luff from Mia *unicorn emoji* *two hearts emoji* *rainbow emoji*

Can I Write

By Mia

How do u no
If ur good enough
To write poetry
It no matter
U write for u
Taking the words
Out of the brain
The feelings
They change as the words leave
As the light hits the words

They shine
They resonate
The brain can see the words
It makes more sense
So I write for me
I make the words
I feel them go from thought
To finger
Tap tap
Letter letter
Feeling feeling
Transformed

In October 2020, Amber started communicating with someone in her head. She assumed Isabel was an 'inner child', had heard of this healing so thought that's what was going on. Isabel was in the dark too.

Isabel expressed dissatisfaction at Amber's life, complaining about many of her choices. She was impulsive, emotionally dysregulated, and angry. Amber spent time talking to her about her feelings, investigating inner child healing, and generally being a lot more patient than any person should have to be.

Fast and hard

By Miya

The heart
It beats too fast
The brain
It works too hard

This next poem is by Mia and Caris. In the future, Isabel will fuse with Cara, who we'll meet later. Together, they are Carisabel, sorry, I mean Caris... Fusion is the process of two or more alters becoming one - sharing all thoughts, feelings, emotions, memories we aren't so sure about, it's complicated how they work. Fusions happen at varying degrees of consciousness, but mostly inside, in the inner world, and depending on the information being shared and processed they can affect those outside, trying to live the life.

Finding each other

By Mia and Caris

When Isabel and Amber
Started talking
It was, more or less
impossible

They couldn't think
At the same time
Information was
Jumbled and incoherent

Amber used
Hypnosis techniques
To help bring
Isabel closer to her

Suggestion
For us
Like everyone
Is powerful

She would count
Ten to one
To bring Isabel to the front

Isabel would count

One to ten
To leave

It took
Months of this
Then after months
Of trauma processing Isabel

They realised
She'd always been there
She was 15 for a long time
Healing teenage hurt and angst

When she aged
She met herself
Found out who she was
Found her true power

We no longer need to count
To find each other

After half a lifetime
Of only feeling each other
Confusing our thoughts
Constant invisible battles

We can now
Talk to each other
Debate
Reason
Love

A couple of weeks after Amber and Isabel found each other, Amber started therapy with a new therapist. Her opening line was something like "I know you probably have things we need to go through first but I've found someone in my head, she's talking back to me and I think I'm crazy". Emma, kindly, told her she wasn't crazy.

It was difficult at first though. Amber and Isabel found they couldn't think at the same time. Isabel would get frustrated. Amber used hypnosis techniques to make things easier but communication was still hard, and often easier to communicate externally, journaling or speaking out loud to each other.

Here is one of Isabel's earliest notes I found:

> "Me and mummy have been watching some YouTube videos of a lady talk about inner child (me). We're watching one about what to do if you get triggered and I'm going to write about it here. Mummy read what I wrote and said that's enough but if I think of anything else that I can add it here any time I like.
>
> The lady says that if you have an emotional response that's too extreme to something that it's being triggered. I get triggered a lot. Mostly about people dying (although mummy says that it's ok I get upset about people dying like Dandan or Hedwig but maybe that if we do some things we can stop it hurting so much so I don't feel so bad inside and cry so much).
>
> The lady says when you're triggered you should:
> 1. Do deep belly breaths. And I should practice this when I'm not triggered too so that it's easier if I am.
> 2. Practice witnessing the ego as an observer. This means I should try to see what has happened and the story that is attached to it so that I can be more rational and respond in a better way. Observe the story and then work out the meaning I'm attaching to the event.

3. Practice self acceptance. When someone is triggered there are internal responses such as hormones and pain. We need to honour the emotions that are coming up and tend to them, to soothe them."

You might be wondering who the hell 'Mummy' is? A big part of healing decades old childhood trauma, is parenting the parts who are still emotionally children. We can imagine how hard this would be for a lot of people, and it wasn't something that Amber took to easily either.

Isabel started calling her Mummy when she was a child/teen, neither of them knew or understood why. Amber told her not to, and Isabel subsequently kept calling her Mummy-I-mean-Amber. That got old quickly, Amber gave up, and now most of the children call her Mummy. When speaking to people outside they try to call her Amber but it doesn't always work. Interestingly, the older alters tend to call her Amber, but from time to time there's a slip and they call her 'Mum' - usually hear themselves, get embarrassed and correct themselves. And Mia's normal way of 'getting' Amber, although these days they're usually both present, is still to shout 'Mummy', repeatedly, in the head.

Anyway, somehow, in spite of the implausibility of the situation, and unexpectedly becoming a mother to herself at thirty-seven, Amber was trying to help Isabel heal as best she could. It wasn't easy though.

"So I was too scared and when my brain starts to panic like at the weekend I can't stop the crying and shaking and just want it to stop and that's why I want to drink or take drugs or kill myself and self harm helps like those things too. It makes it stop in my head when I don't know how to make it stop. And so I cried and cried and tried to make her understand. It's really hard work being so upset and sometimes sleeping becomes too hard too especially when my eyes are puffy and I have too much snot."

They worked through several traumas together, healing them as best they could, as they came up. Events from ages three to thirty. The most significant being a head injury Amber sustained when she was three. I should probably give you a brief childhood back story. Her parents lived in a pub, she was very attached to her grandparents who she saw a lot of and lived with briefly after her father left when she was two. Her Mum moved back to the pub because he didn't want it anymore. Amber's Mum met someone new, he moved into the pub, they had Pete when Amber was four, then when she was five they all moved into a big house in which her grandparents had the bottom two floors and they had the top two.

Alright, back to Isabel, apparently this is about us, not Amber. We are her! Moving on, when Amber was three, her Dad was playing with her and she fell off the back of a sofa onto a big speaker. She had a gash through most of her right eyebrow, the bone was showing, ugh, writing it I can feel it, body memories suck. There was a taxi rank outside so they rushed to the hospital. She had to have five or six stitches. They'd forgotten Tildy though, Amber's doll. She'd scream blue murder if she didn't have Tildy, Nana (Granma's Mum) had not only bought multiple for her but perfected the pattern and made new ones too, Granma thinks there were about eight Tildy's in total. Poor Dad had to walk back to the pub to get it asap.

We're not sure if Isabel existed before this event or she was created then, but the scar through the eyebrow 'belongs' to Isabel. When she's present, it can be painful or itchy. We'll hear soon about Amber learning about the early traumas, this was one of them. She went through it, re-experiencing it in 2019, just over a year before they started communicating.

Throughout adult life, Amber has regularly attempted to be social, just to cry and bail after minutes. Even one time handing gig tickets she had bought to a friend and running! Just to get home and cry that she was missing the gig. Isabel claimed to be responsible for the running, and now we know that she is a protector, it makes sense. We doubt it will have been her crying, someone else will have panicked and been negatively influencing Amber, but Isabel will run in a second if it's going to save someone in her system from pain. Oh, she doesn't embarrass either, and has adopted all of Mia's language choices, just because it's funny. Although, I remember the first time Is met Koreen (a yogi confidante) she was so shy, barely peeked out from behind her hands after Amber counted her out - not the sweary (self-proclaimed) bitch we know and love today!

Auction

By Mia

Does anyone want Isabel?
I've decided I'm going to auction her
Highest bidder wins
Starting bid is 10p
Oh btw
She swears a lot
And will argue about anything
Until the end of time

Isabel suffered with a lot of negative thoughts, as we saw in her journal entry above, which will have always impacted Amber. We definitely don't hear all of each other's thoughts, but bits seep through, and so do emotions and feelings. In December Amber told her Mum about this person in her head. Of course this was strange for her Mum, none of them had heard of DID (it still wasn't even on Amber's radar), so at the moment Amber is just telling her that she's found an angry fifteen year old in her head who takes control when she's been drinking. Yeah, what do you say to that?

The past

By Mia

They say
Leave the past in the past
Don't live in the past
Don't dwell on the past
Learn from it and move on
Um
What about
When ur mind
And ur body
Is still there
And there are people
Who are still
There
In ur head?
What then?

Mia

My birthday

By Mia

Hey
Btw
It's my birthday
Christmas Eve
I'm one
And
39
A week before
And
Se7en
And 4
And 17
And 21
I think
I'll celebrate
As se7en
It's more fun
FYI
I like
LEGO
And
Sylvanians

On Christmas Eve, Amber felt like she 'regressed', finding Mia. Mia was initially six years old. Two days later Mia split, Isabel and Amber 'saw' it happen, Mia was on her way out, seemed to have a crisis over how she was going to speak or present herself and, poof, she's literally mentally beside herself - there were two of them.

The second Mia, shy, introverted, scared, said she would "just be The Other Mia". Someone suggested Maya, she liked it, and our beautiful opposite twins Mia and Maya were born. Mia got younger, and Maya got older.

Twice they've been fused, and together they are 'Miya'. The first time, they were unbearable (imagine the worst teenager ever, hanging around in your head with you) and Amber instructed them to split, after less than two days together, in the middle of a yoga class. The second they had a little more success, but Maya lost herself and they decided they probably want to stay separate, they're often 'blended' together as well, which is similar to fusion but we think less is shared. Fusions feel cellular and in the body, it's a physical thing that happens and can take days and weeks. Being blended, is just hanging out in the same space, not everything is shared[1]*, but you kind of think together, but you can also not. With our experience of fusion (which varies), we can still tune in with all the alters there, but some can get lost when one is a more dominant identity. Mia is - she can carry others, which is what they all need.*

[1] This happened it's too cute not to include but I also can't, so, footnote. ...*not everything is shared it berwoo my musc playing so i writing in the book! ... J: that was Berwoo, she escaped. I don't know what to do with that. Ok. We're currently, at the time of writing, listening to music. I just went to the beginning of the liked songs where all the current music is. Have we discussed how powerful a trigger music is yet? Honestly, it could be anywhere in this book. Music is a strong switch, we can't fight it, and we all have our own songs. She is fighting to come out again. I should change the music. BERWOO WOO WOO. Haha Jessica Embarressed I strong! Woo Woo Woo it my song! Owl city! Im coming after u!! Woo woo woo! Ok, I go. Fank u.*

Mia by Mia

By Mia

So I gots pink hair!
And like unicorns!
And colouring!
And animal crossing!
And my sylvanian rabbits!
And chatting!
And pulling faces!
Amber wastes this face I tell ya!!

In January, Amber spoke to an old friend about what was going on, all these inner children she was helping to heal. Nikki and Amber have been friends since they were eleven and twelve, respectively. Nikki knew about DID, told Amber that she was a dickhead and this wasn't just 'inner children', and linked her to a YouTube video about DID. Amber, Isabel, Mia and Maya sat and watched it... "This is us!!" They'd found an explanation. Step one done, probably hundreds of thousands left to go.

Leave

By Mia

We went for a walk
With an old friend
She says
We make sense
Amber is Isabel
And
Isabel is Amber
Amber doesn't need to be angry now
Isabel can leave

*Nikki gave the system invaluable validation when they saw each other. She knew Isabel. Actually knew her. Stef too, in the future. To Nikki, it was logical, it was an explanation for so many things that hadn't made sense during their twenty-five years of knowing each other. She even says she always knew, on some level, but, when you don't know about dissociation or DID - how can you recognise it? There was a very emotional moment for Amber and Isabel, when they realised just how much they'd hurt Nikki over the years, albeit unwittingly. I can hear the words still, as Nikki tells them "I always wondered, why did she say that? Why did she do that? Is it me? Did I do something?". Yeah, no *all eyes look at Caris* *Caris flips the middle finger and leaves**

It's believed that Mia + Maya = Penelope, as in together they're a different version of her, this is common, for us anyway. Copy, paste, and minus thirty years... But then this one/these two split. Usually it's just age that's variable but we've met non-traumatised versions of trauma holders. And, as they develop, they evolve, they don't stay the same... They have different experiences to their 'original' selves - it's the nature/nurture thing, but difficult to get your head around, because we're different people in the same body. We each live in the body separately, I've no idea how. Pain varies, and energy levels, and we now know how much we feel emotions and store trauma physically.

So, poor Maya took all of Penelope's anxieties and doubts (but damn can she draw!), while Mia, got the other extreme...

First Class

By Mia

Do u no what's funny?
I write like dis
It's shocking at times
And yet
Anuffer version of me
Got herself
A first class degree

In Amber and Caris's words, she's "uninhibited, usually seven, and thinks she's a genius"... Firstly, Mia HATES that we can't use emojis in this book! Her language is variable and absolutely awful a lot of the time, which she enjoys. She also likes to play with language and put 'her own spin on things'; often refuses to (or can't) use the letters R, L, V, and Th; and when others are close and blended, that also can affect language...

This is very visible (to us) in some poems, Mia has an idea for a poem, starts writing. Is all "I C U" and 'no' for 'know', I take an interest, boom the language changes, we don't even notice as it happens and it's only afterwards we're like "oh, wow". So... Basically nothing is consistent, we apologise if it frustrates you, at least you don't have to live with it twenty-four seven.

Mia also pulls 'faces' with the face - to prove she's not Amber. "She wastes this face, she does! Look how far I can bend the nose!" Her way of announcing her arrival is usually just to puff out her cheeks and do some eyebrow jiggling! Granma (Amber's mum), knows Mia. Mia is both new - a fresh start at life, four year old, in a thirty-seven year old body, and is part of Penelope, who we later learned, drove most of Amber's achievements.

Mia thinks how she writes, she struggles to write 'grown up', sometimes can but that's not always the case. We've seen her often fight with autocorrect to spell something wrong. She also age-slides: she can change her age (sometimes) at will but it can't happen when other things are happening in the system. We've had mass 'ageings', where many alters have simultaneously aged overnight, it seems to be related to healing. Ageing changes language, and gait - legs are longer.

And this book would never have happened, if Mia hadn't 'kicked Maya out', and 'became' herself.

Am I Real

By Mia

Disbelief
Am I here
Really here?
What is this
Is it life?
Where am I
How do u no ur real
I feel my fingers
I feel my toes
Breath in my lungs
Air on my skin
Time is strange tho
Where does it go
And where does it come from
How can I be
My name doesn't match
My skin doesn't fit
I cannot see
How it should be
But this isn't right
However,
However
Illogical
It is,
It is

Doubt and disbelief are common with dissociative disorders. It is the nature of the disorder. The brain is programmed to trick us into not seeing each other, to keep us safe. When we switch back in/out - thoughts are forgotten, Mia talks about the amnesia in a few of her poems, it's a constant battle. Here, Mia is also experiencing depersonalisation/derealisation - detachment from herself, her body, even what is real.

Acceptance

By Amber and Miya

Early on
In the reveal
Pre full acceptance
There's just
Is, Mia and Maya

One day
Willow appeared
She's like our grandmother
Wants to help
Amber doesn't believe

The next day
She said
She was making us up
All
Day

I tried to
Get out
But she blocked me
Laughed at me
Said I was her brain playing tricks on her

Isabel
Tried
Amber said

She wasn't real
She was making her up

That night
Amber picked up a pen and paper
She wrote

I am Amber
I am Isabel
I am Maya
And the writing changed
I am Mia

I escaped
I cried so hard
And made Amber promise
Never to say
She made us up
Again

Is and Maya
Called Amber
A f*cking stupid bitch
A
Lot

And now
If someone thinks
'I'm making this up'
Someone else says
'You can't think that'

Mia wants to say something:

This was honestly the worst day we were free and happy and getting to no each other and Amber was horrid! Don't do it to ur alters pls. Work wiff them, dont lock them up pls. That all, luff from Mia. Fank u Jessica.

When Mia 'escaped', there were a lot of tears, and talking to Granma, and a contract was drawn up in the journal.

> I, Amber Louise Ainsworth, promise never to deny Mia or anyone else in the head again. I will always listen and take all of your wants and needs into consideration. If I do not do something right or hurt you at all you can tell a friend or Granma and we can talk about it. Signed, A Ainsworth 23/3/21.

After the acceptance, they were trying to find better ways to communicate and started journaling, a mixture of physical and using the phone's notes app. One of Willow's limited journal entities was:

> "Willow here. Ok. Trying to get some idea of what's going on and sort things out. Difficult when Is/Mia are the only two getting any significant time out.
>
> Still in the dark about what's happening internally. Hoping clarity comes soon. Ugh, thought of Mia and now she's dominating thoughts again. The body needs sleep, but when everyone keeps thinking… W."

They never heard from Willow again... She's around, maybe, but about three days outside broke her and I don't think she'll be coming back. (There's a theory that she was another Penelope in disguise).

Thoughts

By Mia

Awake
Again
Always
We can't sleep
It's hard
The thoughts don't stop
They're everywhere
Waiting
For an opportunity
Scratching
Haunting
The thoughts
They
Jump around
Introspective
Calming
Breathing
And feeling
To
LEGO!
Sylvanian Families!
The music
Gets louder
It's pop
Fun
Others
Wish for peace

Their first, official, minuted meeting involved Amber, Penelope, Isabel, Mia, Maya and Willow, and brought some interesting revelations - some of which would be repeatedly forgotten (mostly anything to do with Penelope). They discussed: managing time in the body, using a spreadsheet to log switches and time in the body (never happened), mapping the organisation of the system, and someone suggesting Amber had been recently tested to see if she could handle the system reveal (no one has any idea what that was about). Penelope's name had floated around before, but no one knew anything about her and someone asked if she would like to introduce herself, I thought it was Isabel she's speaking with but she mentions Is, so maybe Mia, but it could be anyone:

> "I'm Penelope. I've been with Amber since 1986. Loneliness. *Where have you been since we've all been out.* Laying low. Observing. *Were you an alter?* Yes I became one. We were initially friends. Then I became part of her. I comforted her. I took her pain. *Did you know Isabel?* Yes we became friends. Isabel was created after the first head bump. Age 3 apparently. *So Is was first?* Yeah. The head smash open. Amber remembered it when she unwound in the US. She started the process with Is then. Isabel prepared knowing that she'd get here and not know anything that she knew. When others started to show up from the other side. Oh ffs Amber stfu about making this up. She knew she knew fucking what I've lost it. When others started showing up from the other side she started to piece it all together. Amber has another fucking wobble. Anyway. *Is here. Sorry Pen. Right. So yeah. Amber suspected I was related to the head scar. And yeah. That was the no wait maybe Maya's was first? The incident at two. Wtf knows. Whev."*

So this was the first time they heard from Penelope properly, and over the next ten months she would repeatedly disappear, get forgotten about, reappear, disappear, one time they even forgot that Mia + Maya = Pen and decided that Mia and Amber were related (they aren't), she turns up time and time again. The ultimate master of disguise. Interestingly at this point they believe that Maya might be holding the first trauma, wrong again. And you can clearly see in the middle, when Amber starts thinking, Penelope's flow is affected, Amber is starting to doubt again and ruining her train of thought.

The thing, and anger, lots of anger

Sometime around this time, people started paying attention to some thoughts that had been floating around. Amber had always suffered from intrusive thoughts. Wondering what they are? Miya wrote a poem, we're good.

Now

By Miya

Intrusive thoughts
U no the ones
U see a blade
And feel it cut
Even though it doesn't
Or
You look at someone you love
And think
One day they'll die
And I won't be able to cope
And you feel it
Now

Thoughts of self harm or suicide had been common for as long as Amber could remember, but, as per Miya's poem, there can be other ways a brain can torture itself. After becoming more aware of what was happening in the consciousness, they started to notice when these thoughts were happening. When the bad thoughts happened, they'd notice, and box them up. They called whoever was thinking the thoughts either It or The Thing, and for a while just kept boxing them up and shutting them away as they happened.

Until, one day, Mia knew what to do, writing to It in the journal:

> "Dear That Thing. We just want to say that we know you are scared. It will be ok. Being out is scary. It be ok tho fren, just talk to Amber and Isabel and they help you feel better. You can play animal crossing and share my piffle game if you want to! Ok I send you love and hugs! From Mia!"

It was explained to The Thing that they were a persecutor, they're a common and recognisable type of alter who inflicts harm upon the system. This is usually misguided protection - 'if I hurt you, no one else can", 'if you're always prepared for the worst, it's safer', and 'if you kill youself, it won't hurt anymore'. Suicidal ideation has been a constant, we are glad we don't have to live with it (much - things are still rough, and even without persecutors thinking the negative thoughts, it's not uncommon for a quick 'omg can we not just kill ourselfs please?' to pass through).

And Isabel was finding the journal helpful at times, too. Amber had asked for advice from an associate about being open about her multiplicity, Isabel didn't get the response she wanted

> "Yeah, today sucked a bit. Did yoga tf but Mia is ruining smoking. Fucking bitches saying every fuckers a multiple and we're just overthinking it and mislabeling ourselves? Stupid. Fucking. Bitch. Oh stfu Amber gtfo. Yeah ok. I'm still angry. ANGRY FUCKING MOTHERFUCKING SHITBALLS ugh. I maybe wanna try boxing or something lol. K bye Is."

I think stfu is probably Isabel's most used word, not that it's a word. There's a journal entry by Maya the next day that I can't make any sense of, but the last line is just, "Is still angry".

'It' was still angry, too. At some point he chose the name Kai though, there were other names, Kai came later but we'll just use Kai for clarity (inside think that it's hilarious that this I do for clarity.)

Hate

By Kai and Mia

I am scared
I hate myself
I am useless
Ugly
Stupid
I do horrible things
And am not worthy
Of forgiveness
Or life
I wish I could die
I want to do
Horrible things
To the body
I like Mia
She make me feel
Welcome
Even though
I feel bad
And make
Everyone else feel bad
I take away the happy
I make the sad big
I hate
I hate
I hate

I hate
I hate
I hate
I hate
I hate
I hate EVERYTHING
I hate life
I hate breathing
I hate happiness
I hate fun
Fun is stupid
Only stupid people
Think fun is good

Kai enjoyed coming out to construct this poem with Mia from his angry words, and catching up on everything that has happened out here. We don't hear from him often now, he lives deep inside. Mia kept sending the love, as they scribbled at each other.

"Mia: Hi Kai, it Mia. It ok you feel like that. Your feelings matter and there's a reason you feel them!
Kai: What reason? Why I feel bad?
M: It because something happen to you or us. You were very strong and brave and you took the bad feeling for us! We say thank you!
K: That's stupid. I no do that. I hate. I no help.
M: You do help! You do a very good job! You save us and we send you love!
K: I don't want your love!! I HATE YOU
M: That ok. I love you anyway
Isabel: Mia is right, we love you Kai.
Maya: Yep, we love you.
K: I hate you all too. You no love me
Is: That's ok. It's hard to accept, I know. I've felt really bad at times too. I've done horrible things and been full of shame. Now, and yes it's taken time, but now I work with the system, not against it. I give and receive

love. I feel worthwhile. I'm trying to do good and you can too. It won't be easy but you can do it. We promise. You are more than your trauma and all the bad feelings. You can heal.

K: What if I don't want to heal? I don't want anyone talking to anyone outside or inside. I want us all to die slowly and painfully. Horrible nasty. Pain suffering.

M: Ah. That a bit mean but ok if that how you feel. We help you feel better! You keep coming and talking and we send love! You can help me do the house in animal crossing if you wants to? You can have a room! Which room do you want?

K: I want the basement. I make horrible dark and nasty.

M: Ok, but can I put one corner with nice things in? We do together?"

They planned the house, who would have each room. It never happened. Most things planned don't; it's a wonder this book is being written. Ah, it wasn't planned. Except by Mia, anyway.

Maya had not been spending much time out and the others insisted she did, there's a sweet journal entry where she talks about playing some of a Switch game, did some drawing and made and ate dinner. For a long time it was difficult to eat if Maya was close. They never worked out what caused it, but Maya had a big aversion to food. She also didn't spend very much time in the body, so this was huge for her, and she observed she had recently aged which seemed to have changed her relationship with food. They'd noticed that Maya seemed less 'defined' than Isabel and Mia, Is and Mia seemed to be remembering who they were, how they'd always been here, Maya wasn't.

They had questions about Maya, theorising that she was formed when Mia 'kicked her out'. Had Mia expelled parts/wants/likes of herself she didn't want or need? Mia was devastated, of course, but found a positive spin.

"Maya! I love you I sowwy! I never meant to hurt you or make life hard! You are AMAZING! Now Maya can make herself herself, a good and unique position. You do good Maya! Ha love you! Love from Mia and effryone! xxxxxx"

There wasn't much that could get Mia down, but being a child in an adult body can be sad at times, and her headmates weren't always doing the things that needed to be done.

> "I am suddenly and unexpectedly fronting while getting into bed. I realise that the body hasn't done a pee after brushing our teeth. So I go and pee. I look in the mirror and see how old the body is. It makes me sad not being in a little body. So I get into bed and I get my polar bear (he needs a name?) The ear things are still in too! Can no one do anything? His name will be Mr Sprinkle. Oh! I might be older! I think I might be nine! Motherforking shirt balls. I look at the big body and I miss my little body. It's nice to tell someone even if it's only a book! So I go to sleep and cuddle Mr Sprinkle! Goodnight everyone with love from Mia!"

"It's nice to tell someone, even if it's only a book", cute, she told the journal, and now ten months later we are putting it all together, seeing when she first started to realise that most things are better in black and white (or pink and white) than clogging up the already full brain. Oh, 'motherforking shirtballs' - they were rewatching 'The Good Place' (it's good, Netflix).

Words and thoughts

By Miya

There are too many
Words to be written
Most of them don't
Make it out of
My fingers

At night
They swim
Among
Others'

Thoughts

Bouncing around
The focus
Constantly changing

Amber Louise and Tiffany

Happy

By Berwoo

We be
Together though
And
We are
Happy for that

Even when
It's hard
And
There is pain

Mia had been in the 'front'. When she suddenly started crying: "My name isn't Mia! My name is Amber! Amber Louise!" There was a big panic, everyone comforting her, confused about what was happening. Mia/Amber Louise was given hugs and love, and was taken inside. The next day, Mia was back to her old self again, confident that she was, in fact, Mia. There was a new awareness though, someone else was here, and she was very upset. It was over a month before she made contact again though, Mia can tell you:

> "Amber was having a pee and heard Amber Louise crying. She shouted for me and introduced me. AL was happy to have a hug. Amber introduced Maya and Is and had hugs. We went downstairs and Amber

got comfy with cushions and soft toys. Asked to speak to Amber Louise and she came to feel the squirrels. We chatted to her. I was co-con some time. She very upset. Until I showed her Animal Crossing in the head and she got excited and went around the whole island in the head showing effryone (mummy thought her writing until I write effryone!!!!!!!) Anyway. She excite, we agree to build AC in the inner world, me and her go there together! Love from Mia xxxxx"

And Mia was busy having more meetings:

"Mia: Good morning effryone! Should we talk about the contract?
Isabel: Good idea Mia. What would everyone like in it?
M: Mostly that mummy won't ignore us again! Oh, AL wants to say something.
Amber Louise: Good morning effryone. I am Amber Louise. I am very scare. I don't know why. I happy I haff Mia. She make me feel very welcome and tell me I can play! She show me squirrels and let me share them. I love them. And Animal Crossing. I happy I get to haff fun now. I little. Maybe four. I wear bridesmaid dress it blue.
Kai *(most of this is written in upper case. I can't do it to my eyes and ears, but imagine all this shouted)*: I here too. I still very angry but I want to say that I like Mia. She nice even though I am not and I hate. She say I can haff my own game. She ask what I am like. I am a boy. Six maybe. I hate. I want everyone to hide and not talk.
M: Ok thank you AL and Kai. That very helpful. We love you both.
K: No.
M: Yes we do Kai! We love you! You safe! You can play! It will be ok frend.
K: FUCK OFF MIA YOU MAY BE NICE BUT YOU NO NO ME! I BAD! I NO GOOD!
M: That ok Kai.We still love you! Me and Is and Maya and effryone! We here to help.
K: I NO WANT HELP. I WANT DEAD.
M: That's ok. Let's play a game, me and you and Amber Louise. You gotta be nice though. Or else go back inside!"

Mia chatted to him, she asked if he would like to come into the body and play a game on the phone, he said he would like that. She gave him strict rules: 1. You can play the game and only the game, 2. No being angry or thinking bad thoughts, 3. You play the game then go back inside. He agreed to these terms, came out, played the game, was angry he wasn't allowed to be angry (Mia let him have that), and went back to wherever he came from.

Amber's mum and step-dad married when she was four, and yes she wore a blue dress. They'd all been making avatars using apps on the phone too, and in the early months Amber Louise made herself wearing a blue dress. She was getting braver too, popping out every now and then. Always with the leaky eyes. One day, she wanted her 'real Mummy'. They rang Granma, explained the situation, here's Mia's report:

> "Amber Louise came out and cuddled the squirrels. She crying and she tell Granma that her Daddy leave her. She say stuff happen then hurt head. She say she four and younger too. Granma say she older too as five when cold sores. (We think face/nose wrinkling at 4 related to first cold sores). Amber Louise starts thinking about things. Says she understands she's an alter and it's weird, told Granma she loves her 2 times. Oh and I cried because I am 12 and I don't want to talk like a grown up!"

Ugh, getting older sucks, doesn't it, poor Mia (this is something she fights forever, the war against ageing). About this nose wrinkling, all the children did it, or at least most of them. One of the traumas was our first cold sores, you'll find out all about that when Gollum gets here, but we think the nose wrinkling is related to how tight the face was for so long (it was covered in sores, for over a week). Sorry, Mia's report isn't over.

> "AL goes back to the inner world. Maya and Is arguing about who will front, Maya takes it. Says they took AL back inside as she was thinking thoughts they didn't want her to think."

I remember this, it was weird, it seemed like Maya and Isabel knew more than they were letting on. They'd whipped Amber Louise out of the front when they noticed her train of thought, I can't remember what it was though, no one can remember anything, again.

> "Explains that she and Is were arguing and Amber comes back. Feels blurry, hearing things from the other side. Maya came out with confidence earlier, realised she was blended with Amber. A asked M to leave as it felt weird both being in the same space. Maya leaves, Amber says look after the littles please, on her way out Maya turns around and says 'You don't know anything, Mom', in an American accent? Amber was like 'Yeah, I know I don't.'"

I remember how Amber felt with Maya in the same space this time. Sadly, I can't describe it. This was also the first time they saw what happens when the body is empty and people are arguing over who is going to 'take it', as you would expect, it's very much a 'the lights are on, but no one is home' effect.

Mia soon discovered that she could fight ageing, and win. And found someone else, while playing with age...

> "I can age slide! Amber Louise popped out to show everyone Jason dreaming. I thought about regressing to five like Amber Louise and like a minute later I was little and thinking like a five-year-old! Then there was a moment and someone was fronting and they didn't know who they were, they sat and thought for a minute and tried to get Amber but couldn't. They asked what to do and were told to ask for Mia."

Yep, Mia had learnt how to age slide, apparently 'ask and you shall receive' works. They chatted to the new alter and found out that her name was Tiffany, she said she was "the slut in Amber", and that Isabel had been blamed for a lot of things that she was now taking credit for - namely drinking, smoking, and sleeping around.

Eyebrows

By Stef (Tiffany)

I'll always remember the time
I hadn't been here long
Was going to the loo
And I felt Mia trying to get out
I said no
Blocked her
When I walked in the bathroom
My face looked at me in the mirror
And jiggled it's eyebrows at me
That was my first experience
With Mia's annoying strength
It's still weird
When you open your mouth
To say
Something
And someone else's
Voice comes out

Tiffany spent some time out with them, she realised that she knew who she was. She was Tiffany Mitchell, from Eastenders. Eastenders is a long-running British TV soap, and Tiffany's first memories were from late teens, the time that Tiffany Mitchell was on television, and Amber watched it.

Illusion

By Tiff
It's like
An optical illusion
Once you see it
You can't
Un-see it

Maya journaled about the weirdness.

> "Today we had an appointment with the mental health nurse, it went well, he believed us and is going to write to the community support team about the diagnosis. Amber's feeling overwhelmed between the MH nurse believing us and asking questions, and that Tiffany might be a Tiffany Mitchell fictive. We're all a bit shaken. New alter is fine, but the fictive thing is confusing and now Mia can age-slide, and apparently make alters. She made a writer."

Yep, enter me. Mia asked for a writer, and I appeared, ready to write. And Mia had finally worn Amber down...

> "We make Facebook account for us to use!! Very exciting but we need to journal more too! Ok Goodnight!"

There was a little more journaling, but why journal, when Facebook talks back.

Hello world, we're here!

One person

By Miya Squirrel

U look at me
U see one person
U
R
Wrong
I
Am
Many

In March 2021, after the acceptance event, Mia and Isabel were getting restless and frustrated. They wanted to be able to 'have a voice' - be seen, heard, and validated. After a lot of discussion, it was decided they could make their own Facebook account. On the 2nd March, these were Isabel, Mia and Maya's first words to the very few friends they had:

"Hello everyone! Thank you so much for accepting our friend requests! We are aware of how strange/odd/weird/peculiar this is!

We decided to make our own Facebook account, so we can engage with social media and the people that know about us without outing Amber as a multiple... This was the compromise!

Mia and I are the... more extroverted alters within the system, so sorry if we end up posting too often and total rubbish, but this is super exciting for us. So, atm using this account is me, Isabel, I'm 26, Maya is 18 (quiet, shy and creative, we're working on getting her out more!). Mia is 9 or 12 but she's not sure... she keeps ageing which is frustrating her greatly! The tiny little on our profile pic is Amber Louise, she's 4 and new and only just starting to spend time out, doubt she'll be posting, but she's hanging around Mia a lot so who knows.

Looking forward to chatting to everyone now we can! - Isabel"

And, the next day, Mia made her first couple of many, many, many statuses...

"We going home! I gonna meet Amber's mummy and Daddy and brother! And I gets to see my auntie Nikki!! ! I very excited even though effryone else a bit scare! Amber say she dread to fink what it will be like wiff me diving out effry few minutes. I hope we gets to play games and do fun stuff! And walks wiff Jason! From Mia!"

"My best frend Jason and my squirrels! They my favrit! I love squirrels so much that I name our system the squirrel system! We the official squirrel system. I decide as oracle and emperor. uh oh. Amber see. Amber coming. Quick bye from Mia!"

In April, they went back to Amber's parents for the first time since learning about DID and accepting they're a system. Mia can actually be herself for more than just a few minutes. She journaled.

"We are at Granma's! We got here last night and first went into the attic and got a Famous Five book and Eeyore and Tigger and hand puppets then I was a bit shy but felt better quite quickly. We ate stew and dumplings and Peter seem not happy about me I eat the stew tried to leave but was a bit stuck there was a funny bit after Isabel was angry and tried to get mummy but couldn't so she got me and I tied mummies fingers together granma laughed so much."

Amber's brother took a few days to adjust. Sadly, Amber had only told him anything about anything about three days before their impromptu homecoming. I'm not comfortable, Mia?

Alwight so yeah he just didn't like it I guess, thought maybe Amber playing a game? He seemed angy wiff me but then a few days later I was upset and he comforted me and Amber says that something clicked then and he realised it wasn't a joke. He's alright, uncle Pete.

They spent time with Nikki too, one of the first times Berlou came out and spoke to anyone was to crawl around Nikki's living room floor (she didn't want to stand, wouldn't make sense, she was little) to play with a toy shop. Of course, there were tears, all she did was cry, but hugs, love, and toys helped.

I have Isabel's version of events of the finger tying too, just because it's hilarious. She was talking to Amber's mum, and wanted Amber for something, but she couldn't find her... So, she asked for Mia...

> "Poof Mia here. Mia: "I like playing tricks on people. Hmm what can I do?" Looks down, sees the ribbon inside the dressing gown. "I know. I'll tie her fingers together." Proceeds to tie together three of Amber's fingers, before shouting out loud "mummy mummy mummy mummy". - Isabel"

About this method of switching - it's unpleasant for the person coming into the face, if it's talking. So, of course, Mia likes exploiting this for comedic value, you switch in and the mouth is mummy mummying, it leads to some spluttering and head shaking. She even has an Isabel song she uses to get Is/Caris, for the same reason. There was a TikTok "ffs grrr MIA!!"

Even in the darkest times, there's usually a tiny glimmer of humour, camaraderie, joy at being together at last. Usually.

"Best thing about finding out we're all here? So much makes sense!!! Worst thing? We're a we now and have no idea how to function in the world anymore. - Isabel"

Berlou was getting braver, and ready to speak to the world.

Daffodils

By Berlou

I draw some daffodils
It not vewwy good
I tired but I try
Dis is the drawing off my aunti Nikki I do
It bad but make effryone laff
So make me happy
From Amber Louise or Berlou
I like Berlou is shorter
and Ambers mummy used to call her dat when she little

Berlou would like to say something about this poem:

B: Jessica asked if I'd mind her using this status update, it was the first one I did and is significant in terms of my growth and healing. After a long time crying, I was getting braver, Mia's influence was rubbing off on me and I wanted to share within the safe space Amber had allowed us to create online. Mia usually converts the statuses that she feels could work in a poem type form, but I wanted to do it myself. At the time of writing it's December 2021, you should have put dates on, Jessica...?

J: Ugh, really? No... This was April/May time, dates will just be more stuff to clog this ever-growing endeavour up.

B: Are you leaving this conv in?

J: Stop, lol.

B: OH! So yeah, I was saying

Caris: Solid representation of the ridiculousness of this brain, idiots...

B: Ugh, why can't we use emojis? Ok so this poem, I enjoyed spending time with it (and younger me) again. It's 7 or 8 months later, I'm thirty odd years older, have been briefly fused with Amber, and am happy (or as happy as I can be), I feel better than I could have ever hoped for, and we are by no means healed and healthy, yet.

Jessica should draw attention to the fact that the poem above and the words not in italic above are the same alter, as she said, just over half a year apart. I'm Jessica. Oh God, Jessica realises she is narrating herself. Jessica thinks she's spending too much time with this book. Jessica is starting to realise how Amber feels, only she's doing it to herself. Will Jessica include this? Probably.

Sacrifice

By Mia

I often worry
About
The sacrifices Amber made
For us to be us
Me to be me
For this to have
Come this far
The openness
The acceptance
The willing to be weird

It's hard
She says
She hasn't done anything
All she did
Was let it happen
She
She
I know

I'm strange
I'm not like u
I don't have a birth certificate
I don't have my own experiences

Before Christmas Eve
Last year
I have memories of a life not mine
I've had to suffer
It's easier to
Cope with pain
Smol
So I speak strange
And I play
I post too much
I try to
Be strong

And we've all suffered
Amber has lost friends
And made friends
And found a family inside
Separated
By strong imaginary veils
We're here now tho
She lets us be
And yes she's been lucky

Circumstance
Allows
Us time
To heal
Messily

She
Allows
Us
To heal messily
And be seen

Do u no what it means to be seen?
U might no what it means to be
Not seen
It's hard
It creates doubt
Uncertainty
Pain
I wonder how many
Others
Wish to be seen
That's one reason I shout
It's not just see me
But see others

Oh, I see
It took a minute
That's why
She lets me be
She also knows
Suppression
Goes
Badly
Whatever the reasons
I'm grateful
To be
And
To be seen

Belinda Carlisle and Bumblebee

In April 2021, Penelope reappeared, bringing some foggy clarity about who Mia and Maya were. It seemed, she was a non-traumatised alter that had been created, to help Amber cope. Over the course of the lifetime though, Penelope had suffered and often been extreme in her moods.

She was tenacious, clever, and ambitious, but also suffered with doubt, low self-confidence, and self-esteem - and has at times had debilitating episodes of depression. Amber believes she maybe suffers from her own, comorbid mental illness (yep - alters can have their own mental and physical problems, which don't necessarily affect the rest of the system). Penelope's problem might be, bipolar disorder, cyclothymia (faster cycling bipolar), or borderline personality disorder, or not.

There were to be more surprises, about who alters can be. One day, they're listening to music, dancing around the kitchen and cooking. Someone doesn't know who they are, so Mia's in the front, sends her back inside, it sometimes worked that they could shout information to each other. So, new alter inside, Mia shouting into the head "Can you hear me?", "Yes", "What's your name?" "Belinda. Belinda Carlisle".

Obviously, there was some surprise at this. What on earth was happening in the head? Why was there an eighties pop star there? Another newbie can enlighten us, in a journal entry, which shows them finding another surprise.

"My name is AL. I came out a few days ago. Amber Louise was being called AL in the head and when they discussed her being called that outside I was made. I am Amber Louise at 16 or 17.

Belinda Carlisle was found a couple of days ago. At first Amber was confused about how, but then Belinda remembered when Amber used to do Belinda Carlisle karaoke in her friend's living room.

I feel average, average looks, average intelligence. I'm not very clever, I don't have any friends, I'm pretty lonely. I hope I can feel better. Sometimes I don't feel special or nice or worthwhile. I still cry like Amber Louise. AL"

I know you're probably still wondering about Belinda, and maybe Tiffany?

An introject alter is an alter that is a projection of someone outside, inside. They could be based on real people (factives - it's common to have abusers in a system, and they're often persecutors), or fictional characters (fictives) from books or TV. Belinda could remember the shows they used to put on when Amber was about 10 or so, getting dressed up and singing and dancing along to BC. I'm guessing Penelope made her. She doesn't 'front', we think she was just triggered out by music and discovered due to the over-examination of every second in this head. Other than Tiff, who is different to the other introjects who lived inside, we'll find out why later, the only other introject we've ever spent time with is Snape. Obviously, somehow sometime he and Mia became friends. When they do the Mia recovery journaling in the future, he actually wrote in the journal. He's alright, Snape.

And we now had AL and Berlou - same person, different ages. We don't see or hear from AL much; we think she fused with Berlou as she aged. But she expressed an interest in netball early on.

Shop status

by Mia and Berlou

We goin to buy TOYS!
Me and Berlou and Kai
Allowed £5 each to spend!!!
Kai want a Dino or a car
Berlou want a dolly and
I want the biggest bestest doll house you effer seen!!!
Amber say good luck wiff that
From your obvious favrit, Mia

Today we go shopping
For toys for me and Kai and Mia
We go to charity shops
and we allowed £5 each
I wanted a dolly like a baby
We found one
that I luffed but it £15
Kai and Mia said I could haff their £5s
so I could get it
I so happy!
I call her Bumblebee and I so happy I cwy!
Dis her in the pictur
From Berlou

This was a pivotal moment in Berlou's healing, having Bumblebee did something very special, and we've seen the same phenomenon happen with other alters. We think these external toys are created inside, and healing and progress is happening inside as well as outside, all the time. When the littles take their toy inside for the first time, usually we have someone (normally Carisabel) 'hold the door open', the little hugs their physical toy so hard and simultaneously runs inside in the headspace, through the shortcut door we have just to the left of our forehead. Yep, it's weird.

It was also significant for Kai too - he wanted a car or a dinosaur. When he saw Berlou and the doll she wanted so much, he immediately said she could have his money. He was developing compassion and empathy, the others had benefited greatly from having their own friends (comparable equals in other systems - it's hugely healing and validating to speak to people 'like us', especially the children). So they found Kai a friend, I'm just looking at his conversation with James (another system's little). There are some gems:

> "They no let me out cause I fink bad thoughts but dey say if I gud i can come out"
> "I sorry I slow my stinky sister Amber Louise is chatting to a frend too"
> "They just start letting me out bc I mean and nasty. But I don't want to be anymore I fink. I will always be nice to you James. You gud frend"
> "Fank you for being my frend James. We no talk long but I feel better. It's actually maybe nice to be nice"

Kai made fast progress. He aged quickly and now lives deep inside with Cherry and others, taking care of whatever is happening over there.

Amber

In retrospect, Amber says that "If someone told me a couple of years ago I have DID, first I'd have to find out what it was, laugh at them and say "No way, that's ridiculous", and then I'd think about it, and be like 'Um... Wait a minute'". She thought she might have cyclothymia (basically mild bipolar disorder) at one point, and somehow managed to see a psychiatrist a few years ago.

Psych

By Mia

She saw
A psych
In
2016
He said
You have
Depression
And
Anxiety
Lol
Bang on

But, to be fair, when she was showing no obvious symptoms, the system was masked well enough that no one suspected - until Amber and Isabel somehow started talking, after thirty-seven years - it's not surprising no one else could see us. He did note that she had borderline personality disorder traits, but didn't tell her that and she recently found out through the mental nurse. She did always know something wasn't right though.

Explanation

By Mia

She somehow
Never realised
Her thoughts
Weren't her own

She suspected
Examined
But could never find
An explanation

Let's do a bit of history, see where that takes us. So Amber had bumbled through life - she was good at quitting jobs, getting sacked, having significant depressive episodes, various dependencies, impulsive decision making, sometimes a bit slutty. Kinda sums it up. After yet another massive breakdown, wait a minute - she wrote about this years ago! She can tell you... Well, whoever she was in May 2019 can anyway, when she wrote 'Massage and My Mental Health', a blog post...

> "I think I've always struggled with crappy mental health. It's impacted every area of my life - externally: relationships, jobs, school, friendships, and internally: addiction, anxiety, guilt, sleep.
> For a long time I've self medicated with various unhealthy habits - drink, weed, cake, at times self harm and bulimia. If I had a bad day I'd *need* wine, if I had a good day I'd *need* wine, because it was Friday - I'd *need* wine (at times 2 bottles to myself).
> I've spent thousands of pounds on cannabis... Mostly because of "I can't sleep without it", also because of the little relief it brings: when I

smoke and drink enough, I can reach that lovely blackout phase where I stop being me and I find peace, or something."

"WHERE I STOP BEING ME"
SHE KNEW! There's chaos inside.
Anyway, oh, ok, we're being open about the drug use? Cool, I have a poem by Caris...

Mary Jane

By Caris

She's been a good friend
When no one else is there
No one else
Can understand
She
Can smooth
Relax
Ease
The body
And the mind
A bit

So what we also know now about drinking and smoking is that it basically turns us into a roulette wheel. Add shuffled music and we have a party now, but pre-reveal, we assume the dependency/addictive behaviour was a combination of Amber wanting to leave, and others wanting to get out/stay out. We no longer drink after prison, but the other helps a lot - calming, regulating, trauma processing, sleeping. It helps connect us to the body too, and we all have our own baggage in the body, as we'll find out.

Sorry, carry on, Amber...

"It enables an easy mindfulness, where the present is all. I fucking love that place, even when I feel so sick I can barely get up the stairs and have to crawl. Anyway, beyond substance abuse, I've struggled in my own head so much. Sought validation through meaningless sex, been sacked countless times, been a complete dick, cheated, racked up debt, etc, etc."

This is also not just Amber - Isabel, maybe Stef, wrote a lot of this. Interesting. Also, Amber can speak openly about this, without being emotionally affected because of the emotional amnesia. Sad to read though, why couldn't we have found out sooner? Why couldn't Amber have known sooner?

"This is beginning to feel a bit gratuitous, I should get to the point.
In 2016 I had a mental breakdown. There were several contributing factors: Brexit (I'm over that, just ignoring it now), a childhood friend died, I had doubts about my relationship, and 11 years of administrative work that was slowly destroying my spirit (or not so slowly anymore)."

She's had cyclical breakdowns for years, it's been every two years for at least eight, maybe longer. There's a loose theory that the bi-yearly thing might be related to Berlou's trauma, but we've no idea really.

"Shit happened in my shit temp job and my mental health deteriorated. It got so bad I could barely get out of bed. I had flu like symptoms, sickness, pain all over my body, abdominal cramps; the depression was awful, suicide was a great idea - if it wasn't for my dogs I'd've found a way, this has been a recurring theme. Ray is a pain in the arse but because of that he's saved my life many times over, who else would have the patience for that big lump's bullshit?! (That works both ways).
Ben had to take me to the doctors, literally had to help me walk. Couldn't believe it when I came out with a diagnosis of anxiety and a prescription for Diazepam. It helped. I tried to go back to work but within weeks had been unsurprisingly sacked after repeatedly having panic attacks in various situations."

Lol, anxiety. Anxiety is awful, we know, I just lol, because, you know...

"I'm getting to the massage, honest!
Weeks (/months) passed with me on the sofa with my lads and Netflix. Until the eureka moment: I was visiting my parents, smoking a joint at two am, fucking lost as usual, when I started rubbing my sore ankle (I'd hurt it weeks earlier) - that was it! Massage!"

Wait wait wait a minute. This is not Amber! Or this is not the Amber we know now - I can see Penelope and Isabel here but not Amber. Maybe they're all blended, if something is happening the front can get very busy as we become very blended, so it could be that they're all here writing.

"I could do massage! I'd always wanted to do hypnotherapy, but didn't feel like I could with my crappy head. Massage was easy: physical, surely a mental could do that, no? I spent the rest of that night researching my options, looking at courses, establishing that I did not want to go down the Physio route, nope nope nope to full on academia! I found a course at Sheffield Centre for Massage Training that had started a week or two earlier - it was perfect: a one year Diploma in Therapeutic Holistic Massage."

"Crappy head", understatement? "A mental"? Ok, it's no wonder she felt like she was crazy at times, knowing what we know now. And also this behaviour is the same we see here driving Mia's (/my) writing.

"I couldn't sleep and spent the night planning and getting excited. When Dad came down in the morning to get a cuppa, I was straight up there to tell my Mum my plans. It probably came as a bit of a surprise, the last time she'd seen me (about 8 hours before) I was terribly down, virtually suicidal and had no fucking clue what to do with my life. I bounced into her bedroom, high as a kite and having not slept, but actually excited about something - with a plan and ridiculous quantities of enthusiasm. God knows what I said, but I remember her saying words to the effect of "Fine, book it, we'll pay, just be happy!"

God, I miss emojis too, Mia. Wow, just wow. She'd got a plan, kicked Penelope back into action and they were off - overriding the crippling depression they'd be suffering from for months.

> "I spoke with Vicky at SCMT that day, and have no idea how I blagged it but she let me submit an application. I went and met with her the following week to be caught up on what I'd missed, that too went well. I remember her showing me some effleurage strokes (long gliding) and I deviated from what she'd told me, panicked that I might be in trouble but I think I got away with it!"

This is Penelope speaking here.

> "I loved learning to massage. It was by no means an easy time though, I was severely depressed and anxious, an angry vegan, comparatively young, and had joined a group that had already bonded. They were nice, but friendships weren't formed and thanks to my shitty mental health I felt isolated from the group. But the massage was good, and within a couple of months I was off the antidepressants. I qualified in July 2017 and got married a few weeks later. (It was my 'treat' for finishing the course *laughing emoji*) (seriously, how do you type without emojis anymore?!)"

Ok, we share the same brain, I'm convinced now.

> "It's not been smooth sailing since, but finding massage - something I'm good at, that I enjoy doing, working for myself, on my own terms - it's been the best thing that could have happened for my mental health. It's amazing, I can be exhausted and feeling quite crappy, but can still massage. Last year was wobbly but this year things are starting to go well, and I have something that looks almost like a business."

We're pretty sure there is a team of alters who are present when Amber is working - helping her detach from anything going on with herself and focusing on the client, as well as giving guidance and direction. Before she just thought she was really intuitive. And it didn't look like a business for long either, thanks Covid.

> "This year I've got my reiki level two (the internal struggle I had over this part of my practice is another blog!), a certificate in Deep Tissue Massage and Myofascial Release (MFR) with SCMT, and soon am going to America to train in MFR with John F Barnes, the father of Indirect MFR. Life is exciting and fun, I'm earning money and have time to leisurely walk my boys and have the occasional nap. I've been off meds again for 6 months, rarely smoke and have a much healthier relationship with alcohol; I feel good, happy. I'm also getting loads of therapy myself, which is great and definitely helping.
>
> So yeah, thank fuck I found massage, I have no idea what my other options could have been, but this is the best thing that's happened for me since I finished my degree in 2009. It makes me happy, I make people feel better, I help people, and I never have to do a 9-5 again."

Yeah, it's not smooth sailing though, none of it. It was in America that July that she learnt of Berlou's trauma and started digging deeper into what was 'wrong' with her, and just over a year after that that she started talking to Isabel, thanks to Covid giving us all that ridiculous amount of space.

We are sure there is a relationship between Amber's opening herself to spirituality and energy (reiki is an energy healing therapy) and the system reveal. And feel like there is an energetic component to self and consciousness, and experience it as we 'come back into the body', and headspace.

Amnesia

By Mia

Sometimes I think we don't have an inner world
We can't remember

It's just black
Are we just asleep
Or in the dark
But then
I remember the dreams
The places
The flying
The houses
The secret passages
The castles
The sea
The boats
The airport
The diving
The holidays
The caves
The music
The clubs
The parties
The baby animal sanctuary
The mansion
And I think
How do I forget
That I know what I know
The amnesia
Is like a veil
The strongest magic
Interwoven
Between us all
In all directions
We fight to break it
But it is strong

So, Amber headed off to America to go and study myofascial release with John F Barnes, and, as you've seen, I'm lazy, I'm going to let Isabel tell you what happened, in the words that she was directing at John on Facebook in April 2021, while screaming to be seen and validated:

> "Dear John, we just wanted to share our story, and thank you. Without JFB MFR we wouldn't be where we are now, and it's a pretty exciting place we are in. Two years ago in July, Amber came to the US (from the UK) to do MFR I, II, and unwinding. Before coming, she had been on a mission of self discovery and trying to work out what was 'wrong' with her for a while, after suffering with anxiety and depression for as long as she could remember.
>
> While doing your seminars, she learnt of things from her childhood she had forgotten. Significant traumatic events from ages 2-5ish. Since then, she's been trying doggedly to figure out her own psyche while loving practising MFR and helping others with their own trauma.
>
> In October last year we started speaking. I was a voice in her head and she thought I was her inner child. I 'tried' different ages and settled at 15 for several months, we discussed a name for me and I chose Isabel. We worked together through my personal trauma, a head injury when we were 3 years old. On Christmas Eve, Amber spontaneously regressed to 6 years old, finding Mia. A few days later, Mia split, making Maya too. Now we started to look into what might be going on. The 'inner child' theory wasn't working anymore.
>
> We found out about DID (Dissociative Identity Disorder, formerly known as Multiple Personality Disorder). Amber accepted that we are a system in early February. Since then information has come thick and fast. Yesterday we finished an unwind that was started in Chicago, the incident that caused the first split. In the US we experienced what happened after Amber Louise's creation when we were two, yesterday we felt and saw what came before, that made Amber start building amnesiac walls. More system information came through and we

mapped our system (that we know so far). We're up to ten or so alters who 'front'. Know of two/three (myself being one of them) that have aged with Amber and we think we have always thought we were Amber when we are in the front.

Now we have another three months to wait until we see a Psychiatrist for an assessment and diagnosis. Amber is very keen to start working again but we are now a we, we're learning more everyday of how we have functioned. Amber Louise (alter #1) has cried in the head for 36 years, yesterday after the revelations she aged to 7. She is happy, she still has 'leaky eyes' but that will pass. We need to learn how to be us, and now we can be an even better therapist but, 1. we aren't yet diagnosed, there's much fear around the idea someone might still tell us this isn't real. And, 2. if 'we' come out as multiple, won't that scare off clients? But then we cannot be ourselves now, Amber cannot be who she thought she was before anymore, it's a great big mess. We're working through trauma still and want to be functional but there are so many buts! For one we know that I am definitely involved when Amber is working. I understand the whole range of emotions but am mostly unaffected, so I can have the hard conversations without the system getting triggered and shutting down. I don't know if I can pretend to be Amber now.

That's where we are. We need to be able to be us. We're scared (well, I'm not, I'm a protector, I kick ass lol), but the system is. Anyway, we believe that without JFB MFR this may have gone undiscovered. The process of the system being revealed started with MFR. We want to thank you John, and all the wonderful therapists we met during those life changing ten days. Thank you, Isabel, et al."

I didn't interrupt her, that's all I have to say.

Prison

Woe

By Mia

Oh!
My feelings are hurt
Woe is me

This is going to be difficult to do. So I'm going to blast through it. They had to go home. Berlou's trauma was bubbling beneath the surface for everyone and they needed the support of Amber's Mum. One morning, Amber Louise, ugh, I'll let her tell you.

"It's Amber Louise. I am so ANGRY!!! We know now that me and Amber split when we were two. Amber was thinking about this last night, and this morning I was out and cuddling my Bumblebee and thinking about Amber's thoughts and realised what all of this meant. The current accepted theory of dissociative disorders is the theory of structural dissociation. So there is no 'original', we are all parts of one: if you peel and separate an orange, which segment is the orange?

What happened happened and I then CRIED IN THE HEAD FOR 36 YEARS. THAT MAN STOLE MY LIFE. IT IS NOT FAIR. As you can see, I aged. I started getting angry and felt myself ageing. I felt myself getting bigger (I had little legs, and took little steps bc of my little legs and walked fast, even though I knew the body was bigger.) I think I'm late 20s now.

I don't know if it's appropriate to post this here. I don't know anything. We've just been to therapy. I think I want to fuse with Amber so I can be fully present for the rest of the life, obv she says she'll do whatever I need. It's very scary. I just wanted to share I guess. If you've bothered reading all this, thanks. Gonna head out with Jase and stomp around and cry. I'm not leaving the front. I don't think I could if I wanted to. - Amber Louise"

And Mia said:

"YESH!!!! We are going home tomorrow!!!! Home to the body's parentals!! Amber say granma maybe no like that haha Isabel say "she's not my mother"!! Isabel so silly!! I just call her granma bc I call Amber mummy!!!! YAY I EXCITED ME AND AMBER LOUISE GON HAVE A GUD TIME OH YEAH!!! Auntie Nikki we coming for you!!!! I start packing today and so far I know we need a lot of art supplies, bumblebee and my squirrels, and the penguin pyjamas!!! Ok bye!!! From Mia obv bc effryone else crying!! It ok tho, I just do the things!!! I a good girl!!"

They went home to their parents'.

Mia was maybe going to write about what happened next, but she doesn't want to. I could revisit the events but it will just re-traumatise alters and we don't want to, so I'm going to let Isabel's police complaint explain what happened (nothing came from the complaint, of course, but it was something they had to do for Mia).

"We are one person (Amber Ainsworth) with DID (Dissociative Identity Disorder), I am Isabel one of Amber's alters and the individual that attacked Peter (Amber's brother).
I am complaining specifically about the fact that we were taken into custody and placed in a police cell for between 8-10 hours (we think). Amber's parents called 999 asking for an ambulance and help after we had exhibited erratic behaviour (but predictable given everything we have been through and the reason we had visited the parent's home -

working through the trauma associated with [redacted] that happened when we were 2, 36 years ago, and the time that we first started splitting.) Amber Louise (alter #1, made during the trauma) had fitted, they tried to stop us, I attacked Peter, he just held me by my arms until I calmed down. He is 14 stone, we are 9 stone, I wasn't going to get very far. PC H and PC Something arrived as did some paramedics. They spoke to us for 3 hours before arresting us. They were aware of the situation. Her parents told them about the DID, we are not yet diagnosed but did see a MH nurse last week that agreed we do have DID. They had met several of our alters, we were rapid switching a lot of the time and PC Holt had met Mia who is four and very powerful within our system - but emotionally is four years old.

When they arrested us all we could do was try to keep calm. They didn't cuff us because of this but it took a huge amount of effort for many of us to stay calm throughout the van ride to Carlisle and then booking us in. Sadly once we had been put into the police cell, Amber and two other alters went deep inside and couldn't communicate with us outside, myself and some other older alters tried to stay present but Mia was in hysterics and kept coming back to the front. She was terrified, she is four years old but has a 38 year old brain. She tried sleeping but couldn't. They did keep bringing her water but when she rang through crying asking how much longer she would have to 'be in prison' there was no compassion or understanding. She screamed so much that the throat took days to recover.. We hadn't eaten since lunchtime the day before and were brought a bowl of dry cornflakes and black tea at some point (we're vegan).

We should not have been in a police cell. There should have been another option, I don't know what that should have been but now we have an alter exhibiting signs of PTSD (like we don't have enough to contend with), from being in 'prison'. She is terrified that someone will lock her up again."

The only thing I'll clarify is that Amber Louise was trauma releasing, and screaming, their family tried to calm her - not understanding what was happening. Isabel was acting in a blind rage. It's devastating that the event happened and caused a lot of pain for Mia. Initially, as I said, Mia didn't want to write about this. She was reminded how feelings can be transformed, tap tap, letter letter, though, and decided to let it go...

Prison

By Mia

I changed my mind
I want to talk about prison
It's good what Jessica did
Using Isabel's words
So we no haff to think about it again
But I gots to let it go
Bc I'm still scared

It was horrible
The whole thing
Amber Louise
Trauma releasing
Isabel
So angry
Tiff
Amber
Maya
Trying to keep calm

The police talked to us
For hours
And arrested us
They said
Legally they couldn't leave us

It wasn't
Too bad

The van ride
It was about 2am
So quick, no traffic

But the van was horrible
Cold
Metal
Uncomfortable

They booked us in
Amber was there
She was calm
Or trying to be
Amber Louise had gone
She had told the police
What happened
That night
And
36 years ago

Is and Tiff
They were trying to help
Calm

The put us in a cell
We lay down
And fell asleep
A few minutes later
A mh nurse woke us
She was horrid
I was by myself!
Everyone had gone!

She asked me lots of questions
I didn't no what I was doing there
Or if I was in trouble
I was so hungry
She put me back in prison

I tried to sleep but couldn't
I walked around in circles
I kept asking for water
I was so thirsty
And hungry

Isabel
And others
Tried to get me inside
They'd switch out
And I'd just cry
My way back out

I screamed
And screamed
I hit my hands on the wall
I knocked on the door
I asked what the time was
How
Much
Longer

I heard them bringing breakfast
I stood waiting
I said I'm vegan
Maybe an hour later
They brought me dry cornflakes

And black tea
I ate two cornflakes
And drank the tea

I played with the polystyrene cups
My water was brought to me in
Made a pyramid
I tore them up
And made pictures
And played
Naughts and crosses
With Isabel

The policeman said
We would be interviewed
In the morning
Around maybe 10am
I don't really no tho
A police mental person or something
And another nurse
Came and talked to me in my cell
I tried to get a grown up
But couldn't

She said I would be let out
Without being interviewed
I cried
How would I get home
They said they'd talked to Granma
She was coming for me

It was hours more
I tried to be older

I tried to sleep
Eventually I found Maya
She switched with me
They came and got us
Maya can put her head down
Do as she's told
Another police woman asked Maya
About the thing
That happened 36 years ago
Maya laughed at her
Obviously we don't want to do anything
We have a physical memory
And Berlou
From when we were two
I'd laugh at us

They let us go
Amber and Isabel say I've got
Ptsd
I dunno
They may be right
I cried writing this
I get so
Scared
That's one of the reasons Amber let's me do everything I want
I think
I get so scared
Hate being locked up
In the head or in real life

After prison, Amber was missing for a few days - deep inside with Amber Louise and Penelope, processing and fusing. Mia and Berlou (same person - younger version) also fused. It was another few days before Amber worked out what had happened with Mia, she knew something was different, guessed she was using alters or changing her age, but no. This was the first of many fusions Mia went through with trauma holders. When they're fused with her, they can spend time in the front, in the body, healing and living without the pressure of doing it alone. Mia has been our biggest hero. And she discovered the joy of toys...

"We haff had v bad week, I no give big details but awful (Isabel say I v funny saying that!) ... So we just trying to work things out at granmas for a few days. I was out front for days bc I strongest but I four year old so not ideal haha. I haff been bought presents though I got Lego friends and some sylvanian families, I still sad from what happened but it does help haha. From Mia Berlou"

Others tried to help. Isabel spent some time out, conveniently speaking to Granma's next door neighbour, who Amber went to school with... Basically introducing herself and the situation... Yeah, it wasn't good. After that, Amber made Mia second in command - lingually a nightmare, but very present and more trustworthy than Isabel. Everyone was given authority to override any decisions Isabel makes too - we assume anyone can kick her out of the front, stop her doing/saying/writing things still, but she's a good girl now, so that's not necessary. Kai also spent some time out, uncomfortably. Introduced himself to Granma, went for a long walk, did some ageing. And Amber came back, the first of many times over the next few months...

"She is BACK!!! I am so happy!!! She still needs time to recover and feels not really that great but also feels better and is feeling better each day and mentally good and is excited about the future and us learning how to be us and have a good life!! YAY!!! From Mia Berlou"

Memorial

By Mia

I'm so hungry I might die
If I do
I'd like a simple memorial please
Like an 8 foot marble unicorn
With a rainbow gemstone horn
And gold hoofs
I'd like the plaque to read
"Mia. She was wonderful. We will miss her effryday foreffer"
And Christmas Eve rebranded to Mia Day
A day to celebrate all the Mia's

Coming out and Cherry

Strong

By Mia

U c me
U laff
U think she can't be
How can
That
Happen
U
Don't
No
What
I've
Had
To
Do
I'm projecting
I might b wrong
U might c me
And think
Wow
What an ingenious way
To survive
Whateffer

I am me
I am Mia
I am strong

Amber was feeling stronger, or, wasn't 'just Amber' enough that she felt she had to be open. They couldn't hide it anymore. She wrote a coming out as multiple post for her own Facebook account, and sat on it for a few days. Then, we think, someone else got sick of waiting and posted it. It's long.

"This is probably going to be quite long, so TLDR: I think I've got DID (Dissociative Identity Disorder, formerly Multiple Personality Disorder) and am still figuring things out. We are still waiting for a diagnosis, but I think enough has happened that we can say it's not BPD or CPTSD. And it explains a lot about my whole life.

I've always known something was 'wrong', I've been looking for something, trying to fix me, understand why I have seemingly cyclical bouts of disabling depression, anxiety about so much of life.

In October last year I started talking to someone in my head, she said her name was Isabel. It was obviously pretty scary and I am so grateful I started with a new therapist a couple of weeks later who very patiently told me I wasn't crazy every week for months. Isabel was 15 at the time she started talking to me and seemed to be related to a head injury when I was 3 years old. I thought she was my 'inner child' and tried to work with her to heal her trauma.

On Christmas Eve, Mia appeared. She was 6. A couple of days later when she was coming out she split, creating Maya. Mia got younger, to 4, and Maya started ageing, as did Isabel.

Obviously now the 'inner child' theory wasn't exactly working anymore, and when I spoke to my oldest friend in mid January and told her what was going on she quickly linked me to a Youtube video about DID. We researched, there's not a huge amount out there though, and found most information, support and validation from Facebook groups.

Early February I was forced to accept we are a system after a new alter had appeared that I deemed 'too convenient' and denied them for a day. Mia tried to get out to message her friends for help but I just laughed at the crap my brain was doing when I was clearly just faking! She got out that evening and was absolutely hysterical, and made me promise never to say I made them up again.

Since then, some of them have aged, we've found others, Mia's made a subsystem, it's been chaos. Sometime after I accepted it, Amber Louise appeared. She was crying and went back inside for another month or so. Then she came out again. She was the first trauma holder, had split from me when we were two and had been crying ever since. She shared her trauma with us. We've been on two healing journeys back to my parents' since then and in the last few weeks we are really starting the true healing that has been needed.

Myself (Amber, the 'host', and alter that has lived most of the life), Amber Louise, and Penelope (an old alter who was made as an imaginary friend when I was 3, and started to 'take my pain' for me, she is also a lot of my fun and intelligence, she got my degree) have 'fused'. It took over two days and while I was gone, Mia (4yo) did most of the 'work' (feed the body, walk the dog, sleep, play). Very fortunately we were at my parents when this happened so Mia had a lot of support during a very scary time (hosts can sometimes disappear, or go 'dormant' after systems are revealed).

Now we're back in Sheffield. We're trying to settle but a lot has changed. I was hoping I'd get back and suddenly be a functional and productive person, but it's hard. Emotionally I'm all over the place. There's still so much to process. I am now Amber Louise too, and a little is very overwhelming at the moment. I am also Penelope, who we think has been working tirelessly for months behind the scenes while the system was revealed to me. And probably since nearly two years ago when I started to uncover the early traumas that led to us splitting, when training in myofascial release.

So, that's where we are really. We are progressing comparably very quickly but it's still been the hardest thing I've ever been through - I've lost two stone in the last year sitting on the sofa, guess that demonstrates how much stress the body has been under.

Daily life now is me and:
Isabel - now mid 30s and our protector, if I've told you to fuck off or been a dick after a drink it was probably her lol.
Mia Berlou - Mia has also fused with a younger version of Amber Louise (oh yeah, it's like a sci fi book) and the OG is 4yo, she's just got contact back with the rest of her subsystem since the fusions, so will be fun to see how she progresses!
Maya - creative, quiet, shy. She will avoid eye contact and really doesn't want to be around people. But damn the girl can draw.
Tiffany - another protector (that's all I'll say atm about Tiff lol).
Kai - he was a little persecutor, but since he's been given space to grow he's now in his 20s and very supportive of the system (I don't think he has much choice with all his sisters!) He doesn't front much but we'll occasionally hear from him.

Internally we think we are huge. We have a total memory block between here and the other side, fortunately there's very little amnesia in the front, we switch in and remember what's been happening, how I've never lost time (that I've realised, other than after drink) as is typical with DID. In Tiff's words "It's like one of those optical illusions, once you see it, you can't unsee it", which is accurate. It's subtle. I assume I've mostly been co-conscious through life and just been influenced by those inside, or just watching them doing things assuming it's me doing them?! Or I've just enjoyed the break while letting them get on with it at times.

I wanted to be open because 1. I've literally changed, I need to work out who I am now, who we want to be, how to be us?! And 2. No one knows about these disorders! I'd literally not heard about DID until this year, I knew of MPD but that terminology was made redundant 27 years ago. It's estimated that 10% of the population are affected by dissociative disorders, and 1-3% have DID, often they go undetected by everyone as they are naturally covert - they're a survival mechanism. And it's very likely a lot of people have been misdiagnosed with BPD, bipolar, ADHD, etc. I knew something wasn't right, and actually thought all their thoughts were my own, no wonder I could never make a decision. If you've read all that, thanks. - Amber, Is, MIA BERLOU, Maya, Kai and Tiff"

And, a couple of days later...

"I don't know if I ever had any control. But if I did, I probably don't now. Grateful they're all (mostly, pretty much, on the whole) good girls. But life will definitely be more interesting now.

Oh and we've been trying to work out who wrote the coming out post, it was Jessica Squirrel, the writer Mia made when she wanted someone to journal for her (I wish I was joking). She was pretty angry last night that no one had realised it was her for days."

Oh, I forgot that (there's laughing) I wrote it, guess we'll have blended, it makes sense. Tiff changed Amber's profile picture to a poser one of Isabel - very not Amber. Amber was just like 'whatever'. And, being much more open than anyone remembers. Honestly this is crazy writing this book, nearly everything has been forgotten.

"Also that my profile picture is my face but not me is fucking weird btw.
Is: yeah that's bc it's me.
Thanks. I knew that.
This brings a whole new meaning to talking to yourself."

It wasn't long, of course, before someone else made themselves known.

"We gots a newbie! She was triggered out the other day by Lady Gaga! We have some chats and she spend some time out and say her name Cherry. She lots of memories of Gatecrasher and other fun times! We no really do fun for years so she not been around much! She is v welcome to join my party! It all v weird strange this memory front thing I tell ya! From your favrit obv, and Cherry, waving hi to this new world!"

Cherry was definitely a Penelope, she's never had to do any trauma processing and does seem like she just had fun. It's extraordinary how alters bring their own memories with them, we often don't even notice until after, the way when someone (re)appears, we'll start going over periods of the life, remembering events, people, feelings. It just feels like rumination though, until someone says "that's your memory we're seeing now, btw", and we remember what is going on. Early in the year, an ex of ours died from Covid. As alters have come out, who clearly haven't been out for years, they've each remembered him dying and had to go through their own grief. Cherry now lives deep inside, with Kai, and we have no idea who else.

Mia Berlou's crisis

Eclipse

By Amber and Mia

Her sadness
Just eclipses
Everything else

"Mia Berlou is in crisis. She cried for hours yesterday, woke up at 4am crying, is up and trying to not be upset but the leaky eyes just keep leaking. We try to talk to her and cheer her up, but she is overwhelmed by sadness and can't stay away from the front either, in Amber's words "her sadness just eclipses everything else". She's worried she's going to be sad forever. - Isabel"

The fusion was hard for Mia. She had already been through a lot since she appeared four months earlier and feeling Berlou's pain and suffering is one of the worst things she has gone through. Tiff, Isabel, and Amber learnt how to co-front with her. Being in the body together is something that took time and patience to feel comfortable doing, now we can have many alters all very present all at the same time, easily.

Ridiculous

By Isabel and Mia

This whole situation is ridiculous

Thanks for making sure we survive, brain
But this?!
Really?

Mia Berlou was bouncing back, slowly, and as always - a charity shop hunt helped!

"I found dis Care Bear in a charity shop for 50p, I look her up and she called Hopeful Heart. It say dis about her "Absolutely brimming with hope, happiness, and positivity, Hopeful Heart is the kind of bear that will tell you everything's going to be all right in the end. She sees the silver lining around every dark cloud, and knows that no matter how dire a situation may seem, there's always chance to make things better. It takes a lot to get this girl down, but even if that happens you can bet she'll be back to her old self in no time flat." I remember dis and it make me feel a bit less sad. Effryone trying to make me feel betterer and dat so nice I can't belief it really. I do lots of crying but I try to stop now. From Mia Berlou"

They carried on trying to help get her through the worst. I wish I could be optimistic, but it's December as I write... This was six months ago... And it's been constant flux and processing for over a year now.

"Since some time this afternoon there's been two or three of us in the front with Mia at all times. It's been the only way we can help her as she just can't stay in the other side. She's essentially been in the back seat most of the time. She just 'excaped' and called the mother, telling her it took three of us to keep her out of the front, making out we were keeping her locked up. Then she's like 'no, not really', and admitted we were all just hanging out with her because she couldn't leave. Think she's feeling a bit better - I'm fucked if I know who I am right now."

Heavily Isabel, that's who it is, I can tell by the language, mostly 'the mother'.

Fried

By Unknown

My brain is fried
My body broken
Trailing patterns of trauma
Seeping through

This is unfinished, no one is claiming it, no one wants to finish it, but I like it. Oh wow, we're about to hear from Amber, again.

"About two years ago we started therapy. For months I dreaded it for days every week. I would get there, in tears, and cry for the full 50 minutes. It was weird. I had no idea why I was crying, I'd had counselling before which hadn't had the same effect on me but for some reason I just broke in that room. It was awful. And now in retrospect we believe it was Amber Louise, I don't know why she felt safe enough to come out and cry in there. We weren't even the biggest fans of the therapist, but she made something happen.

Now, I think we'd happily have therapy every other day. It's a different place. A place I can talk about all of this insanity uncensored. She isn't trained or experienced with dissociative disorders but without her what we've achieved these last few months would have been impossible.

Today the clinic manager is sitting in with us, he wants to make sure themselves, our GP and the team who will be arranging our assessment are all communicating as well they can and we don't get 'lost'. So yay.

We're also still a mix of people, after finding yesterday it was the only way to keep Mia calm. After spending months examining who I am/we are at any moment, it actually feels nice to just go with it. Know that we're Amber/Is/Tiff/Maya/Mia/someone else in some combination, and realising that this is probably how it's always been. With people moving forwards and backwards depending on triggers, needs and interests."

Ah, she's all blended, that's why we're hearing from her. That's been a repeating theme, most of the times Amber has posted from her own account it's happened while she's been blended or fused with others and it's their influence that prompted the share. Then sometime later she reflects on it and realises it wasn't just her, or reads it back and there are lingual clues.

Anyway, the clinic manager and the exciting sit in, he wasn't there to ensure coordination, sadly. I just wrote this, then found Isabel had written it already! Grrr. Her's is better than mine, she wrote it the same day, I'm doing it almost seven months later. Whatever, here's Is:

> "Therapy didn't go as anticipated, the underlying anxiety was right lol. Our therapist is still in training, and after 8 months of her working with us - working out we're a system, learning to live together, having bloody fusions - her supervisors have decided we're too complex, there's too much risk, so we can't see her anymore.
>
> We always knew she was out of her depth with us, she made sure she only worked with Amber, and it was obvious that was what she was being told she must do.
>
> We've been offered weekly phone calls with the clinic manager to 'keep in touch' while we wait for an assessment. He stressed this would not be exploratory therapy though, but will be working with our 'parts'?! We have no idea what that means obviously.
>
> We're gutted. Emma was amazing, and without her support this would have been so much harder. She gave us a card ffs.
>
> Appointment today with the GPs MH nurse, he's great and hopefully won't dump us. We keep naively hoping one week soon we'll be up to thinking about working again. But after this, what the actual fuck do we do? Atm daily life is just fucking damage control, days are bad or badder. They say the first year after finding out you're a system is the worst, it's gonna start getting easier soon... right...? - Isabel"

The MH nurse didn't dump us. And we were offered catch up phone calls initially, and then the clinic manager took us on himself, thank dog. Our therapy is through a charity, it's not the specialist psychotherapy we need, but it is invaluable and we are very grateful it is available to us.

Mia and Berlou split about 5 weeks after their fusion. Isabel realised it had happened while she was out walking Jason and a new Mia reported it...

> "Berlou was straight in the front and walking home as fast as her little legs could carry her to video call Amber's mum! Mia OG was upset, she was sad they'd not succeeded, she was sad she'd not helped Berlou be happy. But we're good. Berlou is happy, she's still very sad, but is happy she can heal now without making Mia sad. Mia is gradually getting our bounce back. And looks like she can access her subsystem easier now!
> - Mia 17"

Have we even mentioned Mia's subsystem before? Oh there's more confusion here. A subsystem is when an alter has their own alters (like Mia), or separate systems within a system. Mia's alters seem to function as either shells or are blended with her. She can only use them when she is alone and not fused with others (which she has spent a significant amount of her time being).

Amber reported events, too.

> "Thanks for all the kind words and support offered. We're doing better. Mia and Berlou split again yesterday which has helped the system a lot. They were really struggling and we need Mia at her best to get through this! As ridiculous as she is, she helps us so much. We're by no means functional, but better.
>
> We're hoping to start having regular MFR. Without myofascial release, the system might never have been revealed. I'm sure our therapist would say no... it might lead to things coming out we're not ready for... but we don't have a therapist so yeah, we're being proactive ourselves!

We also really want to start writing regularly. Chatted with Andrew Lawes who had some great ideas for a website and a blog! Setting up a website rn seems a bit much but we are thinking we could start a Facebook page that we could all contribute to and any content could be transferred to a website in the future... Not sure yet, there's so much whirling around in the head, but we're not crying and that's all that matters atm - mostly Amber, Is/Maya/Mia/Berlou loitering just behind me."

The Facebook page happened, Amber's Alters, another platform to share from, and one I haven't checked for this damn book! (I'm editing, it's meant to be nearly over). They had some respite I assume, but it wasn't long before more stuff outside of their control was happening. Isabel shared.

"The night before last we had some rough flashbacks, a load of memories from a bad relationship in our 20s. We don't know who they belonged to but it shook us up.

Yesterday morning Amber was really struggling with dissociation, much more than normal. Then she was gone. Mia was in the front alone for hours. She managed well, entertained herself and ate cookies for breakfast in the bath...

She was fed up with it by mid afternoon and smoked, doing the Isabel song to try to get me... walking straight out of the front hoping it worked, it did. I took Jason for a walk. For the rest of the day, well tbh I can barely remember what happened. Oh there was pizza, that was good lol, and Mia played some VR.

Last night as we were heading to bed - don't ask me why but shit always happens in the damn bathroom. We either start chatting while brushing teeth or just dissociate while peeing and realise things. Anyway, Amber Louise was suddenly there - she and Amber split again yesterday.

As per Mia and Berlou's split, this wasn't a conscious decision. It was spontaneous and, we assume, decided inside. So Amber Louise was upset it hadn't worked, we all had a chat and tried to help her a bit. When Mia Berlou split we were shocked - but it worked out well. The time they spent together taught Berlou a lot. She's got more confident (and loves stealing Mia's front which infuriates Mia - "I taught her too well!!!!"). Hopefully that will be the same for Amber Louise.

We went to bed and loads was happening in the head, we actually consciously got to the other side!! Part of it is a house Amber lived in for a few months in her 20s when we lived in Belgium for a bit. A huge old thing with a pool, sauna, library, massive kitchen, trampoline, etc. Seems like a lot of us hang out there inside! It was really busy, there were others there but we can't remember who lol.

So today... um there's myself (Isabel), Amber Louise, and the littles around it seems. Amber's been around a bit but not much, guess she needs some time, as per usual lol.

We've got not-therapy with the clinic manager this afternoon. So we'll go and see what he's about, and we might be back later with good news or tears. - Isabel"

Buzz

By Isabel 'The Tormentor'

Pretty sure
Mia
Gets a buzz
Liking her own posts
We've created a
Social media monster
Oh god she's trying to stop me writing this
Send help!
Now she's shouting
"That's my line!!!"

They were figuring things out fast now, and were slowly making sense of Mia. They knew that Isabel came through in October 2020 as a child, and it seemed like she aged while the system was revealed and met herself in the 'future'/ present... No one recalls there ever being two Isabels - but it is also known that the Isabel that we know now aged with Amber from an early age (we think three, after the head injury).

So, what if Penelope meant to do the same with Mia? But Mia split 2 days later, kicking out a big chunk of, essentially, Pen... creating Maya? So instead of neatly doing what Isabel did and meeting and fusing with herself - Mia got younger and liked being little. Maya aged but also is no longer recognisable as Penelope. Sooooooo.... this also explains Mia's miraculous powers... 'I want a writer' and poof, here I am. I'm just another split/duplicate/clone/alter poofed into existence, from Pen.

Winning

By Isabel and Mia

We sat
Staring in the mirror
Trying to find her
Got a message
She's
With
The
Littles
Remembered a few days ago when she was like
'I just want to hide away forever with my littles'
Guess someone is winning rn

During this time, Amber was missing, on and off - a lot. And often, it was Mia/ Miya who was left 'living the life'. There are many opinions over whether to edit/reduce/not include the following from Miya, but it demonstrates just how hard and confusing this has been for her a lot of the time...

"I am sorting myselfs out. I realise that I feel sooooooo bad bc the Maya part off me (oh Mia and Maya fused btw a few days ago in case u no no,

so now we Miya. There either more off us or I can age slide big time, I no really sure right now, think at least 4 yo and 17 yo. I a mixture now. Anyway)
So now I've just interrupted myself. Anyway. It the Maya part off me is feeling v bad for making me feel bad and so I just spiralling. I haff to break out off it frends!! I NO MY GREATNESS. I just haff to show myself a good time (I no no why inside keep laughing at me when I say that). So I doing the things. I will keep you posted. With luff from your obvious favrit - Miya"

Mia also loves using innuendo, and pretending she doesn't understand it... "I don't! I'm seven!", she says. Doing things was sometimes, normally, all the time, hard.

Motivation

By Miya and Mia

I don't know what to do
I want to do all the things
But no motivation
More than the doing the things
I want to make a montage
Of me doing the things
To Eye of the Tiger
It's now Berlou's favrit song
After Isabel played
Motivational music
To us yesterday
She's got it on repeat in the head
It's definitely not bothering any grown ups
I'm sure

It got better

By Miya and Mia

I had a horrible morning
Front stuck by myself
Forever!
I got very sad again
But then I took Jason out
Managed to find
Isabel and Amber and Kai
We had a nice walk
I made them take photos for me while I sat in the back!
And Isabel made a tiktok to cheer me up!!

In the vague chronology of this, we've just come into June. They've already made their Amber's Alters Facebook page and Instagram account, but Mia has not been allowed to 'use the face'. Amber gave Mia permission to, and then TikTok happened. Amber did give Mia the stipulation 'within reason', which Mia claims to have 'never understood what it means'.

A chat

By Isabel

We've had a chat and decided:
It's not fair for Miya to be putting herself out there
Like this
Alone...
Amber: I'm not doing it, no way
Me (Is): I don't think I should really
Everyone: Tiffany isn't doing it
Looking around vacantly
Cherry: I'll do it
Collective sigh of relief

Cherry never ended up doing much with Mia, but it was sweet of her to offer and we enjoy remembering this dialogue.

Shopping, TP, TikTok

Effort

By Miya and Mia

We shopped without incident
Team effort!
I've played animal crossing wiff Berlou
I gots Lego
And my rabbits
And hoovering
And drawing
And colouring
And change the bed
Now I'm Maya I might be good at drawing
I put bed in wash and then I try drawing
I guess I should take photos off me doing the drawing
In case I do make my montage

Without incident? How could you shop with incident, right? I've no idea when, but sometime when everything was happening, they went to shop. Two shops - a zero waste shop and a fruit and veg shop. They parked, Amber dissociated and left. Maya stepped up and got out of the car. In the queue for the greengrocers, she started to panic. Mia said she'd do it. Managed to get everything in the first shop, she's walking along the road when someone who knows Amber speaks to her. Mia short circuits. Stands, staring at the friend, before blurting out "I'm seven". That triggered Amber back out - fortunately, the friend had heard of DID, and was sympathetic. But it was bad. Ordinarily, when Amber is around, Mia likes pretending to be her...

Undercover

By Mia

I went shopping
Undercover as Amber
She was with me
But I pretended
To be her
My Amber
Isn't perfect
But it is
Good enough

Although, her 'Amber' can be very strange too - she rang the therapist's office the other day "Oh, hello this is Amber Ainsworth I'd like to make a payment please", which triggered Amber to the 'front', who heard what Mia had just said - in a very strange confused child's 'posh' accent - couldn't help laughing but had to recover quickly as she was mid conversation at the time.

Another incident while shopping was when Amber was missing, and Cara went. Mia told her to TikTok it... "I've just gone shopping, and oh my God, someone spoke to me. Turns out that real life talking to people is a bit different to hiding behind your phone social media bull shit. Had a full on panic attack about it, almost. Isabel had to come and save me then she disappeared and then fortunately Tiff got triggered out somehow, I just zoned out staring at the herbs. Fuck me." This is a fun video, for us, not Cara, as she's talking and she mentions Is and Tiff - everything changes, language, posture, she starts out all meek "Hi it's Cara", and then definite Is/Tiff at the end, "fuck me".

There were occasional successes though, as they learned how to live as one. I recall a time Isabel went shopping, it's high pandemic time, and everyone was queuing outside of shops. They're late to go, and are maybe sixth in the line, Isabel was not happy. She was getting more and more angry - with the people in front of her, the people in the shop, the people in her head, the time of day they're there. It's all pissing her off. She could explode at anyone. Amber realises what's happening, switches out and sends her inside. No anger, no frustration, just a few minute wait that really doesn't matter.

Mia's Tik Tok career was prolific, but didn't last long, and sadly her high point wasn't really a high point...

> "So Amber said I could make a tiktok and it was going ok then yesterday I was crying and Isabel took a video of my crying face and made a tik tok of my crying face and it maybe has been viewed 4922 times and gots 448 likes. It no fair. I wanted to be a child star bc I'm funny not bc I'm crying!!! I don't no how to feel abouts this!!! from Miya obv"

Famous because of her crying face, how very sad! (It ended up with over twelve thousand views, somehow, before Mia switched to a private account). Around now, Mia is very much "SEE ME! SEE ME! VALIDATE ME! VALIDATE ME!" (It's the best way to describe it. She has her Facebook account and is collecting friends fast, plus shouting a lot on Tik Tok and their Instagram and Facebook page). When Amber returned to being present most of the time though, Mia's attitude shifted. She started worrying people were only being her friend, or following her, because she was "weird or vaguely interesting"...

> "Also so I think I was a bit hasty adding friends. I wanted lots but now I don't like it. I'd prefer to have five Facebook friends that care rather than sixty who don't or think we're weird or vaguely interesting.
> If you'd like to stay our friend please comment or like and I'll have a cull later. Not so much system friends I know what it's like! - Mia"

She's brutal at times, but at least you know what she's thinking! Her Tik Tok and Instagram were changed from public to private, and she started deleting the people she decided were 'only looking at her because she's weird'. We think she will always have this battle, hopefully it will get easier once this book's been sold and she's a best-selling author, and we're all healed and happy. (You've gotta put it out there! Mia knows what she wants and is manifesting hard!)

Sad

By Miya

I sad today
I no even want to
Make a video
Or play
I would leaf the front
But I no want to
I just be sad
I not by myself
But I sad

Miya split back to Mia and Maya after just a few days. The battle between Mia's drive to succeed, get better, be great, and Maya's wish to no longer be alive, was exhausting. During a yoga class they were driving Amber crazy, and she sent them to separate. They were back a minute later, individual, and much happier. Maya's issues would keep being returned to for many months, her deep rooted anxieties were something that had been with us since we were young, and would take a lot of painful work to process.

Amber was missing, with no contact, for a lot of the summer of 2021. She was inside, waking, healing, and fusing dormant fragments. Alters can't die (not unless the body dies, then we assume everyone dies, at this point nothing would surprise us though), they can go dormant though. And we believe we had hundreds of trauma holders in dormancy.

A fancy word for a big DID system is polyfragmented. This means the system has hundreds of alters or subsystems (it's meaning varies, depending on who you're talking to). Generally, to be polyfragmented, it's assumed the trauma is likely abuse spanning years. We had one bad traumatic incident (we believe), yet we ended up having hundreds of fragments in dormancy - every system is unique, we're dealing with something created by a baby's brain. Cara was ready to rant about this.

"While we appreciate you must have early childhood trauma to have DID, we find a lot of the terminology around that trauma unhelpful... we never thought we had had 'serious trauma' 'ongoing abuse or neglect' or any of the other terms that imply that unless you were abused for years, you can't have DID. We were unlucky.

We had one serious and memory blocked trauma when we were two, but then all the other traumas were just things that happened to kids - head bumps, illnesses, injuries, emotional trauma - all stuff that would not lead to alters being created unless the brain was already splitting! We just wanted to put that out there. Trauma is trauma, and something that cannot be understood as being traumatic to one person, or an adult... you don't know what it's doing inside someone's head - the probability is they don't know either!

Amber's been gone weeks, maybe months I'm not sure. I've not been out very long. She's deep inside healing little girl fragments... we weren't sure if that was true as we don't have good communication with the other side... but we learnt kinda by accident it is. Berlou called her out after being told she couldn't come this morning and she was actually trauma processing! Berlou was scared and felt bad for bringing her out but at least now we know she is inside doing what she can to heal us so we can have a better second half of our life! - Cara and Berlou."

Ah, the Berlou calling Amber and Amber TP (trauma processing - Mia thinks it should just be known as TP from here on) story. Berlou tried to get Amber one day, "mummy mummy mummy mummy", and got the message no - she was unavailable. A while later, she still wanted Amber, she was unhappy with the response she got. She sat down, squeezed her eyes shut and mummy mummy mummy mummied... Amber switched out. She was shaking, rocking, her eyes were rolling around. She stopped breathing and slumped, disappearing, leaving the body empty. Berlou switched back in. Felt terrible because of what she'd just witnessed, but everyone was grateful, they knew now, wherever Amber was, she wasn't just having an overdue nap.

Soon, we'll meet Lolly, Sophie and Jasmine, it's believed that they are the products of this epic healing and fusing mission Amber went on, inside her own head. It was rough, progress was happening, but it was slow and Mia was the strongest and the only one with any (albeit flaky at times) will to live.

> "Hello it's Mia. Sorry for being such a pain to everyone the last 6 months. I don't know where Amber is and it's mostly me fronting so I've aged. I think I'm around 22 but not sure. I've found I can age slide back to little but think I should try to avoid it while I get used to basically being a grown up."

She fights with 'being a grown up' continually. She hates it, and will probably stay seven forever.

> "I've also realised myself and Maya are probably splits from Penelope and the reason she struggles is bc she's incomplete bc I should have aged and re-fused with her but I didn't bc I like being little. So I think Maya and I should probably fuse with Penelope. Which is scary. And while we know nothing is permanent and I know I'm strong I'm still scared.
> The other day I was talking to Amber's mum and realised I'd aged and got confused and then we realised we were Pen and really blended and it did feel very natural. I don't know if I could keep my little self and subsystem. Or Jessica. It's all scary. - Mia"

Aw, bless her, I'm not sure if I'm part of her subsystem, I don't think so. Definitely part of the broader Penelope subsystem though!

> "We fused. Just me and Pen for now, Maya is still separate. It's ok. I can age slide to little but not sure if I should too much. Not sure how I feel, and think this had to happen. That Pen and Amber have co-hosted for most of the life and me being little was preventing that. So yeah."

As you can see, we are pretty good at splitting and fusing. We assume this has always been happening, just no one ever knew. It's a strange sensation, being more than one person. And we seem to use temporary fusions to help each other heal and share information - from every fusion someone has learnt something.

After losing their first therapist, Amber, et al. decided they should expedite their healing and get it over with, and booked a myofascial release session... When it came to the day of the treatment, Amber was missing. They should have cancelled/rescheduled, but Isabel and Mia are scared of nothing and no one so went for it. Isabel got on the table and started unwinding (as we do) in seconds. And Mia was then in the body for about fifty minutes going through God knows what traumas, she had no idea what was happening most of the time. Found herself hanging off the table, pulling littles out of a well in the subconscious (we think this maybe leads to dormancy inside). And Anabel and Abigail were found.

Anabel chose her name to be close to Isabel; she held a second head injury trauma safe and sound for all those years. When she came out, she thought she had angel wings because she thought she was dead. Abigail, we've never learnt much about, she knew her name immediately and hung around with the others, but is quiet, she says she likes reading, that's all we know. And more alters were on their way.

Sometime, Mia and Pen split again, and Mia found her way back to little...

"I'm back!
I'm little!
I been busy
fusing
splitting
finding alters
Gollum a newbie!
Gollum not actually Gollum but like him
She be ok soon
I teach her how to haff fun!!
I been busy on tiktok and playing animal crossing and Lego!
From MIA!!! and Berlou and Anabel oh and Gollum! My little entourage"

Aw, I'd forgotten about Mia's entourage! She normally has an army of small people behind her, and they are affectionately known as her entourage. Cute. So, onwards and backwards, Gollum.

Gollum and Mia's rabbits

She appeared, they were in bed one day when she first came out. She couldn't speak, her mouth was painful, and she was starving and very thirsty - like she was dehydrated and hadn't eaten for days. They affectionately named her Gollum.

They quickly realised she had been a dormant trauma holder, and her trauma had been the first coldsores Amber had around her fifth birthday. Cherry can tell you more:

> "She appears and she's practically feral and Amber's thinking 'this makes no sense, we never had any ongoing abuse or neglect, or anything'. She's like Gollum, all emaciated and can't speak. Then she's hungry and thirsty and tries talking but it's hard. One of the early traumas was our first cold sores - we didn't move for over a week and had sores all over half our face, up our nose, under our chin, in our mouth. Barely ate or drank and didn't, at all, for 3 days - until a doctor threatened hospital and a drip. Someone remembers this and it's like 'omg, that has to be your trauma'. Poor little thing. Like Amber Louise, the first TH. we assume she's just been stuck somewhere."

It didn't take Gollum long to settle with her new head family, and Mia missioned, enlisting help to find her a name.

> "We need help! (Well, obv, but that ain't coming!) We need help less severely than all the other help we need! Gollum needs a name. She says she doesn't want a 'normal' name tho. She wants it to be

something to do with food or water? Any name suggestions? So far the only one we've come up with that she likes is rainbow!"

Their friends were a great help, and Gollum chose the name 'Cara'.

"My name is Cara and I am very happy that my sisters found me and helped me and I love eating food and I like drinking squash too and Mia will show me how to play animal crossing now but I wanted to say hello bc I'm excited to be out. I came out before when Amber was shopping and we got cookies and snacks and I'm excited to eat them and play. From Cara."

Cara wasn't hanging around, being little for long, though...

"Hi it's Cara, so I've done the same as everyone else, just in record time. I've aged and realised I've always been here. There's been quite a lot of "Am I Amber? I'm not. But I am. But I'm not. I'm not anyone else? No. I'm Cara. I'm Amber. I'm um? Who am I? I work! I do massage and MFR with Amber!

Hadn't thought about how old I am... I dunno, maybe 20s, Pen's 25 atm but pretty much invisible bc she's usually blended with Amber really well. That's irrelevant. Also tf my younger self chose Cara. I might have been Gollum or Matilda, or Rainbow..."

Age is weird. As you can see, it changes, sometimes we know specifically what age we are, others it's vague. Right now, I'm in my early thirties, ish, I think. And, of course, it wasn't long before others were appearing, bringing their own traumas...

"Shouting into the abyss that we want information, we want it now and we can handle anything we find out... Had another show up this afternoon, everyone is like WE ARE SURELY RUNNING OUT OF TRAUMA?!There can't be many more?! Lol. Grandfather dying when we were eleven, the day before our first day of big school. That was a fucker. Alex (name chosen after our grandfather) appears crying

"Dandan died" (her name nearly was Dan Dan Died for a minute). In a day or two she'll be good - we are professionals now, I was Gollum a few days ago. *(Oh, Cara, you have no idea what's to come...)* And someone has been recently preoccupied with the idea of Jason dying, we assume Alex has had a lot of if not all grief, so hopefully once she's spent some time out and healed she can quit that! More progress. I'm still here. Trying to be a person and failing abysmally. - Cara"

This is the time Amber was absent the most; it was a relief that Cara was here, adult and temporarily hosted for a few weeks with Mia while Amber was missing. Mia later wrote this poem about that time.

Gone

By Mia

She was gone
For weeks
And months
And while she was gone
I was here
I was seven
I was mostly
Alone
I aged quickly
But hated it
She was inside
Waking
Healing
And
Fusing
Little girl pieces
Fragments
I missed her

Berlou was getting creative though, and, helped by Mia, made a cartoon photo series of what happened to us (she drew, Mia took the photos), she was finding her own way to process and it was amazing. The creativity that has spilled from this brain throughout this entire time has been extraordinary. Amber shared Berlou's picture story.

> "My littles (child alters, the trauma holders) did this yesterday. I keep reading it and being surprised by how much insight they have. Information seems to be coming fast now, we might actually be settling at last. Maybe. Soon. Gaps we didn't even know are there are being filled in. And nothing is surprising anymore tbh."

Other avenues for creativity had been explored in recent months too, including Mia's Rabbits. Mia had acquired a Sylvanian Families campervan and a family of four rabbits. We'd been staying with Granma when she got them, and to everyone's surprise the first thing that happened when they came home was the dad accidentally running over the son and then driving off a cliff. It wasn't the best start, and was the beginning of a very long winded and inconsistent Instagram saga.

Mia's Rabbits later expanded as she first acquired a job lot of figures off eBay (there were nearly tears about their condition, but a wash and some clean clothes sorted them out), managed to get Granma to pay Amber to fix her neck in Sylvanian stuff, and then a friend donated a Grand Hotel, and another two families to the entourage. Needless to say, we're drowning in Sylvanians, oh, and LEGO. Mia also discovered the joy of plastic bricks, after watching the UK, then the US, then the Aussie Lego Masters TV shows, and then rewatching all three seasons of the Australian Lego Masters. We mentioned some obsessive behaviour before, right?

And, because why not, here are the words for the third instalment of the Instagram saga, written by Mia (or, a Mia, or me and Mia - who knows):

"Delia and Simon were playing on their bike and scooter, with Marjorie watching after doing a little foraging.

No one noticed Duncan obliviously heading out to collect some groceries... He didn't check his rear view mirror and BANG! Simon was knocked off his bike!

Marjorie was hysterical! She screamed at Duncan and ran over to poor Simon, who wasn't breathing! She tried to give him mouth to mouth resuscitation quickly!

Meanwhile, Duncan, seeing his dead son and the devastation he caused his family, decided he couldn't cope with the grief. Drove quickly through the campsite, scattering the table and cooking equipment!

And drove off a cliff, killing himself instantly.

What will happen to Marjorie and Delia? Will Duncan and Simon come back from the dead? Only time will tell."

Don't worry, it was all a dream, and then they got lost for years, and now they're in some kind of LEGO Sylvanian nightmare and the LEGO universe and the SF universes are colliding because of a cursed port key, or something like that. The latest wave of littles are excited to restart the saga once we've finished this.

Then there was all the drawing. A lot. Mia and the others made weird creatures out of LEGO and then asked Maya to draw them, sometimes then asking her to colour them, other times they wanted to after she'd drawn it. One of the most striking drawings is Maya's drawing of her anxiety with charcoal. It's scary and sad. There have been bouts of sewing, and someone is anxious to get back to carpeting the Grand Hotel. And, of course, the writing.

We aren't musical, although someone did try to learn guitar a couple of years ago[2]*. But music has been a constant for as long as I can remember. When Cara got here, the music of choice changed, for months it had just been Mia's cheesy pop. Cara was here, and Modest Mouse was back on the playlist. Amber's been listening to MM consistently for about eleven years, as Cara revisited them, listening to the familiar albums - she realised why. He was singing about multiplicity! The more she listened, the more she found... He understood, he knew what it was like, it was no wonder we listened to them so much, we felt such a deep connection to the, often bizarre, lyrics. Same with Twenty One Pilots, he gets it, too well.*

She even started an essay on MM, "'Just being here being you's enough for me" - an essay on why Isaac Brock has DID in Isaac Brock's own words', collating lyrics that were proof he understood. It was abandoned. Caris says she's going back to it one day, when others are allowed to use the body.

---

[2] Mia did learn to play guitar early 2022, after trying to jump in front of a bus, related to processing the big T, and deciding if she couldn't kill herself, she might as well learn to play guitar. Berlou used it a lot to process.

Dandan, part one

"Alex and Cara here. I (Alex) seem to hold grief so it's a bit hard atm and everyone else is missing. Amber and Mia can come but can't stay long. The littles are inside too. We think a lot of walls are being broken down internally, a while ago we got the information there have been 300 fronting alters/fragments over the lifetime and we *think* there might be a mass fusing of fragmented parts happening inside. Not sure why me and Cara are out here alone, but at least we have each other. I guess I just wanted to vent somewhere. I hope the others come back soon. - Alex and Cara"

Mia returned...

"HEWWO!! I back! We ok! Cara and Alex ok, had a big fusion of fragments yesterday and we are TIRED but GOOOOOD!!! Therapy this afternoon so that'll be fun! Amber around! Still expecting the unexpected BUT yesterday was really significant! Cara and Alex did a great job out here even tho they new! We make sure they never abandoned and by themselves again!! From Mia"

Dandan was pretty important to everyone, although, like everything else, some alters had a much deeper emotional bond than others.

"It's me Mia OG 7 year old here I think and Alex who just keeps crying! Dunno where Amber is. Hoping coffee will help us find the grown ups. We gots yoga and we need a grown up to drive us there, from Mia and Alex"

Ok, first, Mia OG 7 year old is one way Mia defines her age, and that she is 'the original' - not one of her own alters. We've no idea who started the OG thing - someone said it, someone else googled it, it means 'original gangster' and Mia thought that was hilarious. Her OG age is her current default age, and is usually seven. So Mia was in a mess here with Alex, confused about where everyone else is and can't find Amber...

> "Uh oh. Alex and Amber fused. Yesterday I was finking I hope I don't haff to bc I don't want to be that sad! We fink Alex is Amber at 11. When Dandan died it was too much so Amber got reset. So it hard. U cudnt make this up. I wish we were making it up then we cud stop! Amber v sad. We cudnt see her for Alex's sadness. Went to yoga and shudnt have gone bc we just cried bc we realised on the way what had happened. Lots of people around the front trying to help but just so much sadness. So Amber says she probably just going to cry until she dies. Which Isabel says is she just being dramatic but we hope the sad eases soon. Just gots to go thru it like effryfing else! Pls send hugs and cake, from Mia"

Mia's optimism and ability to laugh at the desperation of a situation (Mia: there's a poem there!) continues to shine through though... [editing]: she did use 'desperation of situation' in a poem, 'Extra', about a system friend.

> "Amber and Alex together are Amex. It's a laugh or cry situation. I'm trying here."

I'm not sure how or why Alex and Amber split, but it happened sometime after not very long, it wasn't logged, and I think Alex just faded back into the background, and the Dandan grief was boxed back up, ready for another day.

Lolly, et al.

New alters were pretty much just popping out anytime of day or night now, all bringing their own body-breaking memories and trauma. Here, we meet Lolly for the first time (Lola and Leah are other names her various selves have gone by - with Lolly being the child version, Leah teenage, and Lola teen/adult; it gets confusing). Lolly came through specifically holding loneliness, Jasmine not far behind her (sadness) and Tilly/Sophie (tiredness).

> "Oh my dogs. How do you choose a name?! I'm new. Made yesterday awful for Amex and Mia... I assume I was trauma sharing without anyone realising?! Mia was consumed with loneliness most of the day. Then in the evening I realised I didn't know who I was, instead of bailing and switching to someone who did know, I stuck around. Next thing, just like when Mia pulled Anabel and Abigail out of a deep dark well, a little me appeared crawling out of the darkness."

It's common for someone to realise they don't know who they are, sometimes clarity can come quickly, other times they just give up and leave because it's hard work.

> "It's like there are the trauma holder little versions of alters but then we all have our own subsystems? This is so complex. I'm amazed Amber ever got anything done in life tbh. The way we fuse and split, depending on who is close to the front, emotions, wants, needs vary greatly. Unstable much lol
>
> So yeah. Looks like the bottom of the dark space (I hope) is total dormancy, so at least they don't know they're down there suffering while

they suffer, right? When my little self got out she was scared and confused and so lonely. She looked around the room and was amazed by all the Lego and toys!

Then everyone crashed forward to the front and she was introduced to all her sisters and big sisters and got basically initiated into Mia's posse. Sorry, entourage. I'm not crying, you're crying. - currently nameless... I like Freya but can't choose. Maybe I should get with my little self later and see if she has any opinions.

Edit: I've chosen Leah. And my littles self likes Lola or Lolly so that kinda works! This is so weird. After Cara appeared last week she was just out loads. And I'm the same. Assume I'm just thinking the most, we know thinking our way to the front is a thing lol - Leah"

Jasmine quickly followed Lolly, again bringing multiple versions of herself - Jasmine (the little) and Jas (the teen). With alters appearing so quickly and mostly not coming with names, Leah put together a list of potential names to help the newbies! Amber was still often missing and Cara was 'running the show'. It was hard though, and, as we know, even a simple trip to the shops could be almost impossible.

When a Facebook memory of Amber in America showed up, Amber was absent and Cara had something to say about it...

"Ah, before we knew. While Amber was still digging. Trying to work out what was wrong... how right she was lol. Two years ago, here just outside Chicago with John F Barnes and 100+ therapists, she learnt of the trauma that started us splitting. Led to Amber Louise/Berlou crying in the head for 36 years. She also went through one of the head injuries related to Isabel too, among all sorts of other crazy stuff.
It's all so serendipitous in retrospect... The relentless digging... finding myofascial release... starting therapy around the same time... covid giving us space and time to be THIS CRAZY (that bit's lasting longer than anyone hoped, but we are getting through trauma holders like pros now so it has to end sometime!)."

Yeah, no, that was August, the TH's are still coming, now, in December.

> "Looking at the photo, it's like who was that? We think we maybe rapid switch and co-front a lot, because we do now, and assume that's how it's always been, we just didn't know why we were emotionally everywhere at once... it could be any of us. - Cara"

Falling apart

By Cara and Mia

She thought
'I'm literally falling apart'
Someone replied
'No, you're being put back together'

They struggled a lot with Leah's loneliness. Amber was still absent, Cara was trying but finding it exhausting, just keeping it together. Trying to heal loneliness with limited social contact was particularly hard. While Mia, et al. were gathering friends and getting to know people, they still found it difficult. Cara can tell you this...

> "I can't just start messaging her friends like 'Hi it's Cara! I'm not a real person, I'm just filling in for someone (your actual friend) while she's on a fucking rescue mission inside her own head healing the hundreds of fragmented parts that she had to create because that's how fucked up we are! Please talk to me because I'm being influenced by a part that only holds loneliness and it's killing me! Thanks, bye'."

The littles were deep inside too, and Cara was really struggling with loneliness. Mia was around a bit but also finding it very hard. Cara had joined Mia's "When will Amber come back" daily wailing vigil.

Fire

By Cara and Mia

The brain is on fire tonight!
'How do you spell revelent?'
'Is that even a word?'
Course it is!
Revelent!
Revelent!
Why will it not spell?
Revalent?
Oh that would be relevant then.

Mia then got thrown back in at the deep end, and was fused with the three teenage trauma holders that were hanging around. This fusion didn't last long - Mia is an unbearable teenager, add in three others who are each suffering in their own way and it was a bit of a nightmare. They were struggling to find a name - Mia finally chose 'Moody Mia', which the teens weren't too happy about. They were finally processing though, Cara was no longer being constantly affected by Leah's loneliness, the Mia/Jas/Leah/Thalia fusion meant a change of direction emotionally, and Mia was finding anger. So that was fun, I bet.

One morning, Cara was chatting to a system friend they had made. Cara was talking about the trauma sharing that was going on, and these people told her we were doing it wrong, that alters should never share trauma outside of therapy. This threw Cara, she didn't know what to say and assumed they kinda knew what they were doing, questioning everything Amber and the others had decided over the last few months. She panicked.

Amber and Isabel hit the front, Amber seeming more maternal than ever, making the fast decision that we shouldn't be talking to that specific system as there was a significant age difference (which she had been uncomfortable about, but Mia and Maya had made friends) and their approach was very different to ours - they were getting regular, trauma focused therapy. We don't know what we are doing, but are trusting we can work out (most of the time) what is best for us and what the system needs to move forwards. Perhaps if we had had specialist psychotherapy, the processes might have been different. We were doing the best we could.

Amber went back inside, carrying on with her in-head mission. And Isabel stayed... And stayed... And stayed...

> "Isabel's been around most of the day and damn that is hard work! She's amazing and so strong but who can be bothered to be that angry? We know now that she basically gets triggered out whenever there is pain or fear so she has had to be that strong, but still.
>
> Our friends suggested she should *maybe* work on her anger and she was just like "uh no, we've got more important things to be doing, my anger is waaaay down the list, I've decided". I think she's attached lol."

Argh! This is so cute, in a few months, they'll be (hopefully, permanently) fused. Isabel had some more work to do on herself before she and Cara could be one though. And while Cara is a little 'lost' in the fusion, when we check in with her she says she's happy and 'feeling strong'.

> "Amber has been around a bit. It's interesting, a theme in yesterday's therapy was 'more' she is more. She says there's still some days' work inside. I asked for an eta and none came so I guess it's not easy!
>
> Amber said it's becoming more complicated inside as they're now onto the trauma holders who are dormant so they need waking up and healing then fusing with another alter. We think Amber is taking a lot on herself which makes sense."

Ah yes, we believe Amber has done a lot of the work inside, working to process traumas and often choosing to fuse trauma holders with herself.

“We had another teenager appear in yoga this morning. She just likes netball?! We had a think about who she could fuse with bc she didn’t seem complete and decided AL might be a good fit. So hopefully that might be good for them. AL is a teenage Amber Louise/Berlou... She’s not been around much that we’ve seen, might be a lurker though lol. I’m still here. Glad Isabel’s left me. Just keep going until Amber comes back. As per the 1000 times we’ve already said this... You couldn’t make this up. - Cara”

Months later, Berlou must have met and fused with AL and the mystery teen, because suddenly she wanted to play netball! Isabel actually takes her to play netball! You’ll see. And meanwhile, Mia was still Moody Mia, and it wasn’t going very well...

“BORED BORED BORED. Seriously. How long can someone mission in their own head?! This is silly!!!! We try to fill time but we are just waiting for Amber to come back!!!! Graarghhghhhargh. And physically we seem to be falling apart now too. So that’ll be part of the healing crisis ridiculousness we are currently in the middle of!

And we get jab #2 tomorrow so pretty sure that will hit us hard bc we are a mess but also trying to be positive bc if we assume it will be crap we risk just making it bad bc we thought it will be?! I’m still a moody teenager and it SUCKS. I hate you all I do.

Gonna go slam my door, stamp my feet, and be passive aggressive FOR EVER. Cara says no lol. Ugh. - Moody Mia (I removed the rainbow from my emoji signature bc before it represented hope and that we would get there but c’mon. Realistically we will never be a real person that has a real or even happy life. We’re destined to be eternally miserable so no more rainbows, I accept this. Berlou says I should stop being dramatic! Well she should just go.... Uh oh. Isabel’s gonna get me. I’m going I’m going.) BYE I HATE YOU.”

Like I said, good times. Mia was back to being Mia soon though and this fusion only lasted a couple of days:

"Mia's back. Berlou came out earlier, likely sent with the message for Mia to split from the teens. First thing after crying Mia OG 7yo did was check in with the littles. She got each in the front and made sure they were ok and coached Tilly (who we don't think has fronted before other than a brief cry) doing her journal page. She's gone back inside to rest. Haven't yet heard from the three girls but Mia's magic is usually very powerful so whether they're one or three we're sure they'll be doing better wherever they are. This is exhausting. Heard from Amber, no news just a weak hi and check in. - Cara"

After the fusion the three teens did stay together for sometime, and chose the name Kali. They stayed together for a while, until their little counterparts healed and aged their way up to them and other unities were required for progress... Mia had this to say about the fusion.

"This is my bad joke... that makes zero sense to 99.9% of people... As someone who has been fused a great deal of times I can decisively say that Kali (a fusion of 3 trauma holding teens), is the worst people I have ever been. And I only spent 2 days with them.

Yeah it's bad, I know. But so right, I was fused with the three teens (Thalia [Soph], Leah and Jas) just for a couple of days to get them used to fronting and heal a bit with my magic etc. They then chose Kali as a name when I split from them.

Like we had a bit of knowledge about Kali in the head but dayum (apparently I'm working on my American too, I have no idea what's going on. Cockney, American, 7, 12, 20?! Berlou is floating up and down age wise and I think we're connected and I'm following her!) ANYWAY. I did a google obv finally. (Wiki) "Kali is the chief of the Mahavidyas, a group of ten Tantric goddesses who each form a different aspect of the mother goddess Parvati." WHOA HOW DID THEY KNOW BC THAT AIN'T IN THE BRAIN!

Alright see ya! - Mia!"

And...

"Mia 7yo is swearing after spending two days with three teens, in a bad cockney accent too. - Cara (assuming now that this cannot possibly be real and at any moment I'm going to wake from a dream)."

And...

"I've decided I'm going to have a welcome home party for Amber. It Mia. Bit tired. Teenage is yucky hard and no one shud ever haff to do that! Anyway, I haff no idea when she be back or we strong enough but who is coming to my party? We do something fun. No alcohol obv. Amber heard me planning this b4 and came gave me a hug and said sorry and she be back as soon as she can she just busy and weak atm too from effryfing she doing inside. From Mia"

When Amber did come back, one of the first things she said was "We aren't having a welcome home party!" But this is one of the sweetest things, Mia can be so very pure and naive at times. Mia is the hero in this story, actually Mia and Berlou are the heroes in this story.

Party time!

By Mia

Oh the parties in the head!
The revelry
The celebration
There's permanently noise
Right behind us
Everyone is so excited
Her mission is over
She's back
Where is my golden unicorn though?

"We think we've done it. Well Amber has done it. (Amber: no we did it. I did not do this alone, if we have "done it"). She's been mostly inside for weeks and months and it's been so hard. She's been processing trauma inside, healing and fusing fragments. While outside we've had crisis after crisis with trauma sharing, fusions, splits, insomnia, it's been constant and awful.

Amber came back a couple of nights ago. She's tired but strong and present. We don't want to get our hopes up too high, but this, now, might be what we've been waiting and hoping for. There's a calmness.

We believe there are now a lot more alters we do not yet know. But are hopeful now, that the inner world has been restructured and amnesiac blocks altered to allow if/when new alters come to the front they will know what is happening and know who they are. *Hopefully*. There is so much busyness behind us but it is a buzzing, excitement, not the usual "oh crap, what trauma is coming our way now?" "Who's crying/ wants to kill themselves?"

We know things won't be easy. But we have ALL our fingers crossed that we are right and this IS what we've been waiting and hoping for. - Cara, Mia, Berlou, Amber, and everyone else here in this head"

Amber came back, yay! While Mia was busy trying to get Instagram/TikTok famous, Berlou had been healing and growing, and had her own plans - she wanted to save the world's trauma holders! A few days passed and they seemed to be settling. Knowing just how fragmented they were, and how difficult that would be to heal, there were big question marks about Amber's mission and it's success. Could someone really mission inside their own head, healing little pieces of little girls? Berlou always had concerns, she had fears that there may be others still suffering inside their own head, she knew it could happen. One day, though...

"Berlou was in the front last night and got the message 'No one was left behind' she cried so hard! It's such a relief. We still don't want to hope too much that this is what we were waiting and hoping for but it really feels like it!
Berlou is sooooo emotional about this, because, ridiculously, she still blames herself. It was her trauma that caused all this and she's so relieved that it's over (we hope!)
It seems she's the only trauma holder that suffered for any length of time. All others went straight to dormancy until they've recently been woken, traumas processed, healed and fused appropriately. After Berlou, the systems that we have had in place were made. They were over vigilant it seems though which is how we became so fragmented!
Berlou is currently planning on creating a YouTube channel to try to help other littles. My TikTok has been fun but it basically turned into a video diary for ourselfs and while I'll still do some bits I think this idea is a really good one!
Fingers crossed. I'll get my golden unicorn damn it!! - Mia"

I read this, see the optimism and hope, and it's weird - they're managing huge healing, but in the scheme of things there's still a lot further to go. Unpicking 36 years of life can't be done in a quick few months' work, sadly. Progress is progress though.

Mia's happy Amber's back, well, everyone is happy Amber is back. They're still constantly trying to work out what is going on inside their own head. Harry Potter has been a constant comfort for them since they were in their mid teens. Amber's brother was reading The Prisoner of Azkaban. Someone here had a look at it, and within a few days had read the first and second books and were fighting Peter over the third! We've watched the films I've no idea how many times, and the books we've read maybe five or six times.

Since the reveal started, we have no space for 'new information'. We are rewatching Friends again (Isabel did last year, too...) and read a bit of Harry Potter occasionally. Before the reveal, Amber used to have a few books on the go at any one time, we now assume that was different alters and interests varied depending on who was around!

They're playing around one day, trying to work out how it works, moving forwards and backwards and communicating with each other, when Mia announces that where we are when we are co-conscious is actually the Room of Requirement, which makes a lot of sense - we're working with a space which isn't limited by the physical, we believe our inner world is heavily Harry Potter influenced, and magic works over there! At times we've needed some real life magic.

So, with alters and where they can be, in relation to the outside world, we have:

- *The front - this is where we are when we are in the body, we are in control. There can be more than one of us here, and we can share the space quite easily (as long as everyone has the same objective anyway - someone would really prefer to be playing and it's actually becoming a bit uncomfortable for me to carry on, and now I've noticed and addressed this I am very aware of the frustrated little people who want to play with their Sylvanians. I guess you'll still be here later). (I'm back, kids have played).*
- *Co-consciousness, or co-con - this is where we know what's going on outside, can (usually, we think) communicate with the person fronting, and can easily 'switch in' to the body. There are different levels of awareness though. It feels like this is right behind the eyes.*
- *Access to the inner world is behind there, but we do have a shortcut to little land though, which is just to the left of the head. As we go deeper, awareness of the outside world subsides.*

The way the amnesia works though, any movement between the front and the Room of Requirement can lead to a dissociated state, and whoever is fronting might forget what's just been going on. We can also move between places, just to forget again. I've no idea how we do anything tbh. We've tried to consciously 'break through' to the other side, a lot, but we either get thrown off track and distracted (not hard), or fall asleep.

I haven't talked about switching either. Anything can cause a switch - seeing something, hearing something, thinking something. We know that a dangerous thing to do is 'tell someone else's story' - half way through we will switch, not realise and it's only when the person fronting speaks about themselves in third person, they realise they've switched. We assume this is how it's always been - Amber gets close to remembering/thinking/talking about something that 'belongs' to someone else - switch, amnesia means nothing happened, memories are there, just foggy. Music is a strong switch and we can't fight it. I had a battle with Berwoo somewhere in this book because I had her music on. Her additions were too cute to delete and went in a footnote. Now, if you address any of us, regardless of who is out, we would probably switch. The person fronting may be disgruntled if they were doing something or mid-thought though!

We're in July, and Berlou has just made her first YouTube video. She had aged to 12, and decided she wanted to make a YouTube channel to try to help other trauma holders. She made her first video. No-one could believe her bravery, strength, and determination to help others.

Amber gave Mia and Berlou Special Medals of Commendation for Services to the System, at the moment they're just in the head. This had much more meaning to Mia and Berlou than Amber expected when she said it, one day we will get them their medals (a unicorn for Mia, and Berlou wants a squirrel medal.)

Oh yay, here comes Tildy...

> "Hello it's Berlou. We have been visiting Amber's mum and dad for a few days, so much has happened that even Mia hasn't done any social mediaing. We figured out the puzzle of our system, who the illusive and powerful alter is that made Mia among other things. It was a shock but

made total bizarre sense. I'm by no means healed or fixed but I am feeling better, I did some deep trauma processing last week. We're heading back to Sheffield today. I'm starting a bucket list, Mia wants me to make it a thing but we'll see, it's hard, I was inside for a long time (as were others) and we really feel like we are starting our life again together. I'm so grateful to have Amber and all of my sisters and our parents. Yesterday I took myself to Ullswater to paddle and Aira Force which is a waterfall. It was lovely. So many of us feel like we are experiencing life for the first time. It's special. - Berlou"

The Magic Doll

This new alter, no one expected, and was much weirder than Tiffany Mitchell, or Belinda Carlisle. Cara and Is wrote about it and shared in a Facebook DID group (Mia found it in the notes). This was too weird to share with friends, even for us.

"We've been deep in this trying to work out wtaf happened to that two year old to cause this... there have been so many puzzles and we knew there was someone inside with power we just couldn't work out who!

She finally showed herself to us a few days ago. She'd said she was an imaginary friend and started 'taking Amber's pain' when the system was first accepted and we were at a loss - no one here nor Amber's mum had any memory of there ever being an imaginary friend.

So... we never saw this coming, even though we should have... it was a doll. We knew that we were hugely attached to this doll for years. Amber's mum thinks there were about eight Tildy's, bought and made by our grandmother. We do remember screaming when we didn't have her, and now it makes complete, total, bizarre, incomprehensible sense. She was an alter, she did take our pain (dormancy was full of little girls she basically just put to sleep, hundreds). We understand now why we couldn't cope if we didn't have her? It's just mind blowing.

We can also see how a lot of people just couldn't get here. Let go of what we're taught to believe as adults. Accept that a system is something that was made by a child's brain. We were two, there's barely a sense of self by then.

We just wanted to share. If you're looking for answers, they may be more obvious than you expect lol. We're exhausted. It's been relentless for months. Trauma sharing, fusions, absolute chaos. We hope now we can settle. - Cara and Isabel"

Yep. A doll. A magic doll. As we saw, Amber started making amnesiac blocks when she was very young, and as such the brain working out the processes was quite immature... When looking at DID, and other disorders caused by childhood trauma, rationality can't be applied - the brain that constructed the coping strategies didn't have language or logic!

Tildy was so tired, so battered and bruised and worn out, so scared she would be rejected. And she sobbed so hard when everyone embraced her. Over the next couple of days, she got weaker, she tried to 'go dormant', and everyone rallied around, trying to work out how they could help her. As we mentioned, magic works in the head. Mia led the ceremony - intention and suggestion, a bit of faith and belief, and you have magic. They managed to transform Tildy, who couldn't be in the front or the body - it didn't work, she wasn't human - into a real little girl.

The first time Tildy 'fronted', and was able to look around at the outside world, they were sat looking at the view from Amber's parent's garden. It's pretty epic, overlooking the fells around Ullswater in the Lake District. Tildy was so overwhelmed, she couldn't believe she was real, present, truely in the body. She cried and cried while we sat with her. I'm not sure what happened to her, but I am tearing up thinking about it, I think she has, oh, she's here. It's Tildy, I thought they'd forgotten about me, I didn't think you needed me anymore. I'm a little girl again, maybe I could be friends with Berwoo and Ray of Sunshine? Definitely, welcome back Tildy. We thought she was living deep inside, everything is so confusing. People can get lost easily, and the littles tend to be in pairs of 'best friends', so no one gets lost.

With all these memories coming up, piecing together what happened over almost four decades, they had to find an outlet, beyond Facebook. Now, with the appearance of Tildy, they felt like they could take a guess. Maybe they could write a children's book? Why not? It started well, look:

"When you're two, things aren't quite the same as when you're thirty eight. And when you're two, sometimes it's hard to know where you end and other people or objects begin. Sometimes a doll can become much more than just a doll. Given the right, unfortunate, circumstances."

We wrote, pretty consistently, for a couple of weeks. Until Dandan part two happened, we wrote about the grief, and didn't look at it again for many months. Anyway, we now have an army of littles, who are all getting braver, and wanting their own validation, there's Lolly:

"Hewwo! My name Lolly and I now Lady Lolly Littles Leader! Mia and Berlou big now so I in charge haha! I did this drawing of Mia in her pink castle wiff her golden unicorn! I don't no much about myself yet but I happy Mia and Berlou are my sisters thank you from Lolly."

And Little Cara, Jasmine and Tilly (she changes her name to Sophie later):

"Little Cara! She like pink and helping people! She 4-6 yo and like Lego. Jasmine I like Disney and want to be Disney princess and I wear princess peach dress! I no sure how old 5-7 maybe. I like purple. I Tilly I choose dolphin and I like blue and the sea and I 5 year old. That us! We happy!! We gots sisters and excited to play! Hewwo to all the other littles!!! From Lolly and effryone here"

After everything they'd been through, they were about to have one of the biggest scares yet, Amber stepped up, asking for help and support from Mia's Facebook friends:

"Mia's weak. She's been getting weaker for days. She has carried us for months, healed many trauma holders, kept us going when everyone else was ready to give up. She's sung, TikTok'd, shaken this ass, done ridiculous things with the face. Accidentally made a subsystem from doing accents and voices. She's loved us all and been incredibly selfless throughout the last 7 months since she appeared on Christmas Eve last year. She felt like she just needed to fuse with everyone, and while we maybe should have just said "ok you've worked hard, do what you want"... we can't. Berlou and her are inseparable and we aren't ready to not have her here. I can't believe I'm the one here writing, this is their social medias lol. And I can't believe I'm sharing what we all just wrote to her. We aren't letting her go. She can't front and says she feels like she doesn't have a body (lol - someone was like um yeah none of us do?!). Please, any kind words to her would be so welcome. We are so close to restarting our life and we don't want to do it without her. Thank you. - Amber (she's so SM motivated I'm hoping this will somehow help... we just want her back)"

In the journal they have, in which each alter had a page which was being filled up with stickers by big little fingers fast, they had written to Mia, words of strength and encouragement. They did magic, soaked in salts and lavender, drank magic tea, and prayed like they believed, thank dog it all worked - I don't think anyone could do this without a Mia!

"Alwight! We back. We good. I'm weak but being looked after. Amber is planning on starting work again soon so if anyone wants to come for a freebie next week she's hoping to do a few MFR sessions at home! She thought we just ask on here bc less people and only people that know us and said I could cause I not done any sm for ages!

Yup, it's Amber. Obviously she can do whatever she wants now, so here we are. Everyone inside is so excited, it's so funny, for years I've said that it's amazing - doesn't matter how tired or what crisis is going on but when I start working "I feel like a different person"... now we understand why. I know Cara is a heavy influence in my team of therapists inside, and think I know who else might be, can't wait to get hands on people and see what magic happens tbh. If anyone has free time and would like a session let me know. - Amber"

This was way too premature for them to be starting working again, but ten out of ten for trying. They carried on, mostly suffering but it wasn't all bad. It was decided that Amber wouldn't be having another birthday - she had had them all so far, and this year it was Berlou's birthday. Berlous was struggling, since they'd nearly 'lost' Mia she was all about the tears, again. If she was happy, she cried, if she was sad, she cried. There was still a lot more healing required.

Let's hear from Amber again...

"Obviously with getting ready to work again I've been thinking about working... I can't believe how blind we've been to being multiple. Only a couple of times have I heard a voice that was not mine tell me what to do... "only a couple of times"?! Like I'd been exploring my spiritual side and just attributed it to my 'higher self' or something? That maybe should have been a red flag in retrospect.

But more commonly I'd just find myself thinking about doing something, we all thought in the same voice so I guess I hear someone think about something/direct me and just follow that thought."

And Mia also had big plans...

"WE ARE GOING TO THE LEGO SHOP!!! I will advise you of any purchases later! Luff from Mia! (Lolly, Tilly, Jasmine and Carabel want me to mention their legocitement too)

Grrrrarghararagharaaaa!!! We chose to come to the Lego shop on the day there's loadsa new Star Wars stuff out and there's a three year queue to get in!! We have found some jeans that fit though (there was a lot of indecision so Tiff came out to sort us out quickly) and gonna grab some Lego from Argos instead! Berlou is LOVING looking at things and the littles liked looking around the Disney store! From a disgruntled Mia!"

Ooh, the looking at things thing - everyone likes looking at things! When Isabel first started coming out and communicating with Amber as a child/teen, she would sit and look at all the things around the living room, remembering their histories. It's a common theme, especially with those who have been inside for a long time. There are a lot of memories to catch up on.

Speaking of which, memories. We share a lot, but it seems there is emotional amnesia around a lot of things. Previously, Amber was able to speak about sensitive/painful things related to other alters because she wasn't affected. With access to memories though, it seems to be that you need to know what you're looking for. I can't just go poking around without knowing where I'm going.

Although a lot of memories seem to be shared, they aren't labelled "Amber", "Isabel", etc., so working out who did what when isn't easy, either. However, it's common that someone quite new out will notice themselves revisiting periods of the life, and we've concluded this is their own memories bubbling around closer to the consciousness.

It's the same with the front, we can't just walk out here, people have got lost and turned up weeks later. Berlou has recently learnt to 'think herself out'. We have no idea how any of it works, maybe one day we might have a better understanding but for now it's all weird and crazy. Anyway...

Miaism

By Isabel and Berwoo

She finds and pay for her Lego in Argos
She's sat waiting
Her number is called
She goes to the desk
The man says
"Thank you for waiting"
... this actually surprised her

She replies
"Well, I didn't really have many other options"
Says 'thanks', etc.
A minute later
"What else was I gonna do?
Pay for my Lego and leave without it?"

Lego is a constant, now, I'm afraid....

"We've been back to the Lego store! Had such a good week! Done a couple of treatments, started writing our kinda autobiographical children's book - it's so nice to write nice words not just status updates, hopefully therapeutic and cathartic too as we're going! Jessica Squirrel will be the author - handy as she can easily write about Amber/us in third person! And the littles love it too as it's like telling them our story?!

We're working on having daily plans of 'must do' things - 1. Play. 2. DBT workbooks. 3. Writing - either the books or website stuffs!! Amber's gonna be open about the (assumed) DID from her business pages/ website - which is scary but she wants to work with women with trauma and we sure know about that! Everyone says you should have a niche - and Amber thinks anyone that would be put off by our experience probably aren't the clients we want anyway!

Nice relaxing weekend now before more treatments and being a semi-functional person next week! Wooohoooo!! That concludes your Mia update for today!! Hope everyone has good weekends and find time to playyyyyy!!! Luff from Mia!! (and Lolly!!!! I here!!! I like the Lego too! and Tilly and Jasmine and Carabel! Yes yes all my entourage want to say they here too!!!)"

She's hilarious, I love her, and this...

"The worst thing about Amber being back ALL THE TIME is she keeps making us eat healthy!! It not so bad tho when she makes us nice fruit salads! I basically spokesperson for our system. Wanna talk to Amber? I can make u an appointment if u like!! Oh she says no that is not how this works! Whatever."

They kept going, plenty of LEGO playing and trips to the LEGO shop. They were lucky they could be working through this without the pressure of work or (real) children, and the little contact with the outside world that they did have was really just getting to a couple of yoga classes every week, and therapy.

Amber has been going to Hot Yoga Commonside for about seven or eight years. I remember when she first started going, she looked at the yogis and this little community, and thought 'I wish these were my friends". Well, she manifested it and most of the friends we have now were made through yoga or massage! Throughout all this chaos the HYC studio, it's heat, lovely people and energy, has been crucial to their healing. Koreen (HYC owner) will be included in Mia's acknowledgements, I'm sure, but without having that space where anyone can walk in and be seen, heard, validated - well, it's priceless (actually it costs the price of membership haha but ok - Mia). They've cried about the unbelievable things that have happened this last year, been through so much in that room. Sweat and tears, a lot of, while they've been shaking the trauma and anxiety out of the body with wonderful yoga and wonderful friends.

One day someone saw a fire ceremony event, and signed up for it. It was forgotten about (everything is forgotten, at least twice). And on the day they got a message about a change of location. Only because it felt like a last minute 'Ok, we're doing this!' did they get there. It wasn't great, but could have been much worse.

Amber dissociated and left after not long at all, so Tiff took over, in Mia's words giving "zeros poos about the fact half the room didn't know about us and was just like 'Yeah, I'm Tiff'". The fire ceremony aspect involved writing things you wanted to let go of and burning them. Berlou did this part, finding the strength to speak in front of around eight people about her intentions. After the ceremony, there was plenty of food so Mia was bouncing around, Cara and Tiff chatted to some people. Berlou came to the front though and felt socially isolated, she wanted to join in the conversations others were having but just didn't have the confidence. She wandered around the studio, and the tears came. She just wanted to be seen, but she couldn't make herself known and was beginning to panic. She grabbed her bag and ran to the car, where she broke down. Amber was able to switch with her then, and took her back to say goodbye to Koreen.

This happens a lot, and is the opposite of how logically these things should work. If someone is in the front and gets upset, they can easily shut everyone else out. Others could be trying to communicate with them or switch but it's like there are blinkers on. What would have been helpful here is if Tiff switched back out, barged her way into a conversation and then had Berlou be either co-conscious or switch back. But, it doesn't work like that. (Some comedian just said "Answers on a postcard, if you do know how it works, please.")

Berlou was struggling.

> "I've been feeling pretty bad today. Amber was meant to do a swap treatment this afternoon and then rescheduled it because of me. I wish I could just be better and feel better. I wondered before if I could just go dormant bc everyone else is all ready to get on with their lives and I'm holding them back. A couple of days I managed to stay away from the front and that was better for people but it seems like we can't really control it and it's mostly been me here today. Everyone's been looking after me and I started to do the DBT workbook that we got. I'm going to do a few pages every day as I really don't want to make life bad for anyone. Also after Amber rescheduled her appointment a man rang her who Amber worked with his wife a while ago. He needed someone to talk to as his wife suffers from a dissociative disorder and I'm glad we were free to talk to him. I hope we've helped him and her even if it's just a little bit. Sorry I just wanted to share. Thank you for reading, Berlou."

This is so sad to read, but you can see here, while she's still suffering and finding life hard, all Berlou wants is to help others. The DBT workbook got abandoned after not long, but Berlou got through enough of it that she was able to start making conscious choices about her thought processes and responses.

> "Hello it's Berlou again. So last night I came to the front and immediately got overwhelmed and was crying and couldn't cope. I remembered the DBT workbook I started yesterday and even though I haven't got to any of the things about how to cope or what to do when overwhelmed I wondered what it might say. So I focused on my breathing and body and Mia broke through and gave me cuddles and then Isabel and Amber and others did too and I've been told I'm banned from the front by myself now. What happens for some of us is when we're upset we get stuck, doors get shut and we're all alone. It's weird. So anyway Mia says we're conjoined twins now. We don't want to fuse but she says she's not ever going to leave me alone. Today we just have therapy this afternoon. So I'm getting up soon and going to do more DBT workbook and we'll carry on writing. Amber just needs to make a couple of phone calls this morning but says she will take going back to working as slowly as I need it to be.
>
> Isabel's not been around for a while and Cara already had to stop her from... um... being herself (?) on Facebook this morning (pretty sure she was about to start getting unnecessarily sweary). It's funny they really balance each other, and their little trauma holding versions of themselves have fused and are Carabel and they're really happy together too. Thank you again for the support and kind words. - Berlou"

It's like we're reading a Isabel-Cara love story, except the end goal isn't a romantic relationship, but a pairing that balances them both, and makes life much easier for everyone.

I'm worried that I'm killing this book with status updates but we're seeing Berlou grow here, and the interactions between alters. I can't paraphrase or sum this up. I dunno. Mia is gutted she's lost her book of poetry - so we need to print that too, please, someone.

> "Soooo... Isabel hasn't been around much and it's funny bc even though she's horrible me and Mia really like her (I can feel the scowl)... so I started to do some of my DBT workbook and suggested maybe she do it with me... it was so funny how differently we respond to some of it - she got angry with the book and called it a dickhead bc it was asking her to think about coping skills we might use even tho it's not told us any yet!
>
> "If you would have taken action in this situation, what might have happened?" Isabel: "I have no effing clue, you tell me dickhead" is what she wrote. She might be a lost cause!"
>
> I'm feeling much more positive about the future. I know it won't be easy but I want to get better and be able to regulate my emotions and responses and be able to be (part of) a real person!"

Berlou's trauma was coming up again around this time. We were writing a lot (just for a change), and Berlou decided to write about her trauma in detail. She did, she contemplated sharing it. And decided to share within a Facebook group. She typed it up (it was handwritten), and sent it to the group. Fortunately, this particular group approved posts before publishing them. Half an hour passed and Berlou started panicking - what if someone read it and it hurt them? Did they even really ever want to speak about this? More importantly though, what if it hurt someone? She went to the group and managed to delete the post before it was published. She deleted every copy of it from the phone and computer. She took the paper, the original, outside. And without ceremony, burnt it. It was another step of her healing, for Berlou.

Dandan, part two

We don't know who wrote this, or when, but we found it in the notes, I'd guess it's Mia Alex. Mia considered converting it to poem form, but she doesn't want to edit it...

> "Dandan. We miss you so much. We wish you had been here with us. We loved you so much and we know how much you loved us. That's why it hurts so much. It's like a vice around my chest. The grip of grief. The consumption. I miss you. I wish you were here. We wouldn't recognise each other though, you've been gone so long. Eleven years together. Twenty seven apart. I can still see your hands and hear your voice. You gave us a safety that can't be replicated. A love that we felt so deep. That when it was gone, the void was too much to bear. Without you in our life we've suffered. We needed you and you left us."

They got up one morning, the usual four am unable-to-sleep routine. They came downstairs, got some tea, and started to write, continuing the children's book that I started. Realising they should be writing present day as well as thirty years ago simultaneously, wondering what this might mean for their book, if it might change it. They were coming up to Dandan's death, and as they started to write they allowed the tears to flow. It was strange. The pain, so familiar to Amber but also fresh and new, with an intensity and freshness, like it was yesterday. They moved forwards in time, to yesterday. They wrote:

> "They'd triggered Alex back out. They knew she'd been in there, they knew she was resisting coming to the front because she knew then,

then they'd all need to feel it. She would have to share her pain and she didn't want to do that to the rest of the system. They embraced her though, as they wrote. Giving her the space to share, and release her burden.

Another friendship was potentially ruined as Isabel was close to the front, impulsively lashing out. Blinded by their consuming pain. Mia and Berlou were still connected, Amber was very present, the front was busy as people moved around, allowing themselves to feel Alex's pain and move through the healing process.

They went to nap, and when Mia woke a little while later, she and Alex were fused. It wasn't a surprise to Mia. It had been a few weeks since she'd last had to go through a fusion with a trauma holder and she embraced it. Sobbing for hours. Letting Amber and the others look after her/them. After a while, she and Amber spoke. They talked about what they knew about processing trauma, this pain felt different to Mia though. This pain was all love.

It was so strong and so powerful because the love between Amber/Alex and Dandan was so strong. Mia sat with it, feeling it, honouring it. She noticed where she could feel it in her body. She drew everyone's attention to it. Shining a light on the tight restrictions around the hips. The heaviness pulling, weighing her down. She felt the dull heaviness across her shoulders, deep in the centre of her back, wrapping forwards, around her chest, into the solid lump of her heart.

Mia Alex even hypothesised that grief was thicker, it's density within the body actually weighing more, that maybe gravity had more pull on it. She saw how debilitating it could be."

Thank you, grief

By Mia Alex

Grief is funny
It doesn't hurt
It dulls and pulls
Takes the joy
Gravity is stronger
You can feel it weighing down your heart
It pulls you down so you can't see
The colours are duller and the excitement gone
For why enjoy when it can't be with them
Muscles feel heavier
Unable to move
Disabled by the pull down
Down down down
As the body sinks into the emotions
The heart drops further
Feeling like an iron block
The mind sinks down too
It doesn't see it happen
It slows and stops
Unable to cope
With the heaviness of the body
The sun might shine
But it matters not
The grief doesn't care
It just keeps pulling
You have to fight
See the joy in life again
Appreciate the colours
Fight the heavy, grey, blanket of grief
Honour their memory

Thank them for the time you had together
Promise to never forget
Even though you know that would be impossible, anyway
Carry the grief like a testament to them
Keep it safe but contained
Thank it for always reminding you of the love you had together
And treasure it
Give it space and time
Indulge it when it shouts too loud
Open it up and allow it to breathe
Let the air and light in
Acknowledge it
Become it
Embrace it
Feel it so deeply that together you are stronger
For it is your friend
It wants to be with you
It wants you to look after it
It wants you to treat it with the love it deserves
It remembers and will never leave
But when it speaks to you
Reminds you of it's pain
Say thank you and remember a happy memory
Feel the love and share it with the grief

They spent the day focusing on self care. Dandan said he hoped she would remember him. Painfully isn't how he would have wanted it. He'd have wanted them to remember him with joy and love, appreciation for the time they had together. Easier said than done when it was twenty seven years since he died and memories were still scarce and patchy. She could feel his love though.

The next day, well, after their first sleep and waking at two thirty am, and getting up to write less than an hour later. Mia Alex tried to access his memories. Found she could actually see his hands. Feel his arms around her. As they wrote they sobbed.

"They listened to the music Berlou had been playing and crying to for days. Not fighting how the music practically drew the tears out of their eyes. Mia Alex looked again at her grief. She had noticed the day before that the pain was a different quality to other trauma pain. She had realised it might be something they had to learn to live with, not something that could be healed and let go like some others. But as she paid attention to it, still gently sobbing, grateful Jason was there with her. She found it didn't have the same density as yesterday, maybe it couldn't be healed or taken away, but maybe with acknowledgement, time and love, maybe it could change. The brace around her heart, it felt more lattice-like in it's consistency. It wasn't the solid lump it was yesterday. She went back to bed, hoping that when she woke in a few hours, it wouldn't be quite so consuming."

Shine

By Mia Alex

I took
Grief
To the kitchen
Put on
My music
We danced around

We made
Sweet potato fries
I told her
That really
She's just
Love

U don't need to
Feel so heavy
She could
Feel lighter
Be brighter
U are actually LOVE

She felt guilty
For feeling happy
That's ok
But
He wouldn't
Want u to

His love
Wants to
Shine thru u
Not dull u
She said
Ok

They'd pretty much processed Alex's grief now, and Mia and Alex didn't stay together much longer. There was no respite though.

"We just take it in turns feeling poo and it rubbish. Will this last forever. Amber feeling all bad and I try to cheer her up and that she's not even trying to stop me doing this shows how poo she feels. We went out and watched The Greatest Showman yesterday and late home and maybe that just exhausted her. It was hard as she had to try to stay in control and also let us do what we wanted to do. It so hard. I wish I cud make her feel better. I been listening to music she likes and made her a cake but she just sad. From Mia Alex and Berlou"

I'm sorry

By Mia Alex

I'm sorry
It's just one thing after another with us
I'm sorry
We have 36 years to process
I'm sorry
We don't know what we're doing
I'm sorry
I overshare all the time
I'm sorry
I haven't been strong enough to magic us all better
I'm sorry
If you're sick of reading about us
I'm sorry
I'm not coping
I'm sorry
We are suffering
I'm sorry
We're grieving something that happened 27
And 36
Years ago
I'm sorry
We're a useless friend
We have no space
To see outside of ourselves
I'm sorry
I feel so bad
And I don't know how to not
I'm sorry
Simple things aren't simple
I'm sorry

I want to stay motivated
Believe it will get better
Tbh
I'm sorry
We even exist today

Amber was clearly struggling now. Isabel and Cara stepped up and took control for Mia while Amber was processing whatever she was processing!

"Isabel has managed to hold the front for a few hours to give her a break, Amber just needs a little time and she'll be back. I guess us other "grownups" (lol. As if any of us are) have been used to her being around and taking care of the littles and daily life so have been a bit lapse! This journey... it was never going to be easy... but we'll get there. And one day (hopefully sooner rather than later!) it will be so worth it! - Cara and Isabel"

And someone finally realised that the reason Amber was such a mess, was that she wasn't alone. She had fused with Maya. I'll let Mia tell you more.

"Is and Tiff got us to yoga and it was good! Them and me and Berlou got super into the body and moved a load of stuck stuff around! At one point Isabel did look backward in the head and ask what was happening and saw Amber and Maya wailing and carrying on so there was a big SHUT THE DOOR SHUT THE DOOR panic! Sometimes these amnesiac barriers can be helpful!"

Occasionally the amnesia and lack of understanding anything that is happening, can, as she said, be helpful. Amber and Maya spent five days together; five painful, debilitating, anxiety filled days. There were triumphs though:

"Tiff and Is also managed to do shopping and pretended to be a normal person successfully - Mia Alex and Berlou!"

So, all this is still going on, and Amber is somehow still on a mission of starting work again! Cara was exasperated, I think is the right word...

"Of all this ridiculousness... today is somehow the most surprising... (um no lol - Is) we have two new clients in an hour. First ones since like October. Amber's not been here. Just says entertain yourselves, I'll come back to prep and go and do them. ALL OF US are like wtf are we doing?! Shouldn't we have rearranged them?! There's so much anxiety and even Tiff is questioning this and she's pretty unaffected. Either Amber knows what she's doing or she's legit lost the plot, unsurprisingly. I expect Mia will be here later celebrating or we'll be a jibbering mess. Or both. - concerned confused Cara, Mia Alex says send help (Amber's just noticed this and is facepalming, quick, post!)"

She did it, somehow learning to detach from whatever chaos was happening internally and start focusing on others (a bit, sometimes), again. This is a repeat theme from here - others sharing her body, trauma processing, going through their own personal hell, and Amber just letting them get on with it, scheduling clients and somehow scheduling her own time, in the body, mostly unaffected by the everlasting pain and suffering (someone says I'm being dramatic - I'm not). Mia Alex can tell you more.

"Amber did her two treatments and BOSSED IT! (she also says she thinks this is the first time anyone in this body said bossed it!). They absolutely loved it and want monthly treatments! So fine Amber knew what she was doing and it turns out she wasn't just inside resting yelling at Cara to entertain herself, and me and Berlou were inside with her doing some healing magic! Berlou is feeling better too!

Yesterday we rested and saw mh nurse. He did some of the SCID-D test which is a test for dissociative disorders wiff us just to see and that was interesting, Tiff isn't a narcissist and Isabel isn't THAT antisocial! We did get good scores for histrionic and borderline and another one tho unsurprisingly!

> Amber and Maya spent a lot of time feeling their anxiety and being with it which Amber said was strange as usually she avoids it or pushes it away. They did some trauma releasing then Maya wanted to draw and drew where she feels anxious. It's a funny picture. Pretty but sad."

We haven't mentioned the mental health nurse we see monthly much. Amber spoke to a doctor one time, asking to be referred to the Specialist Psychotherapy Service, he said no, but did suggest we see the nurse. Obviously, disgruntledly, she accepted (any help is better than no help, right?) It was one of the best things that's happened for us. We have about an hour with him once a month. Anyone can walk in (Mia often does), and he's been so much help. Having someone who knows what we're talking about, that we don't need to explain all this jargon to. And there was the wonderful time Amber asked him if her experience and presentation looked like DID to him, he laughed at her "Yeah, it's DID". He is also invaluable in the future fight for a diagnosis.

Positivity

By Mia Alex

Positivity is discarded
I give up
They can't fight the anxiety
She is just used to it
Heavily present
Utterly useless
Debilitating
I wait
For time
To pass

Amber and Maya's fusion was one of the worst times they went through, the anxiety affecting everyone within the system as Maya shared. Finally, they got through it though, and at the end of the processing, realised it was all old abandonment trauma related to her absent father. This was the status that became one of Mia's first poems, you might recognise it:

"Feeling better Amber laughed at me for always sharing and wants everyone to know I'm not part of her we are both part of this not that I am her we are both part of the same thing but separate and now she says she was only kidding that I should report that information!!!! Graargaragaragh. We think Maya's finished sharing. She and Amber have split and feel better. Realised I maybe had to feel it all so strongly too bc we maybe were the same person until December and I pushed her out and then became my wonderful self, unrecognisable from who I was before and hence so ridiculousdonkus. So whatever anyway you're all stuck with me now (I'm talking to the rest of my head) k bye. I'm gonna play with Lego. From Mia Alex"

Tiffany/Stef

Stiff

by Miya

Tiff she was
Hiding
Behind a mask
Off TV
She pretended
Even
To herself
That
She was
Someone
Else
Shame was
Scratching
Her
Behaviour
Had
Often been
Questionable
Super slut
Extreme
Like the rest
Of us

Fortunately
Amber
Holds no grudges

To explain the 'Off TV' part... As we mentioned earlier, there are different kinds of alters, and some of them can be fictive introjects, from any source. When Stef first appeared early 2021, she said her name was Tiffany Mitchell, and she was an introject from Eastenders (a British soap). The earliest memories that Tiffany brought with her were from our mid - late teens, which made us believe she had been created then. When it came to Tiffany's personal healing journey, we learnt the persona was a mask for who she truly was. One thing that wasn't mentioned earlier, with prison. So, Police Constable H, he looked a lot like Grant Mitchell, Tiffany Mitchell's on-screen husband. Tiff hit on him, he was quite pleased with himself while telling Amber's Mum about it...

Stef and I wrote this for the children's book as she was going through her own personal healing crisis.

"As they lay awake during the early hours the next morning, Amber thought of an old love. Wondering where he is and what he's doing, she did a little Googling, searching various social medias for him. All of a sudden, the thought hit her, "Ok, who's influencing me now?!" And she realised it was Tiffany. She'd known Tiff had probably hosted for a while at that time, noticing in retrospect the changes in behaviour and even a brand new wardrobe.

As they thought about what was happening now in the body, Tiff came to the front. And was stuck. Physically she felt awful, with heavy solid pains in her chest and around her hips. Tiff realised she hadn't actually felt anything for anyone, even herself, since she had her heart broken all that time ago.

She felt herself grieving a relationship that barely even started 14 years ago. She felt herself becoming vulnerable. The next day she was still in the front. The others were around and they had some communication but whenever anyone switched in they just switched back out within a couple of minutes.

The others all tried to tell her to soften, feeling into the body, the healing, the life. But she fought and fought. Determined to quickly work out what it was she had to learn, remember, feel, to be able to leave. By day three she was getting increasingly frustrated. Sympathy was little from inside, she was angry with Amber for even working out they had a disorder! She wished she could just retreat back to wherever she was when she wasn't here.

That evening. Someone who thought they were Tiffany, spoke about Tiff in third person... This is an odd but good indicator it's someone else, we don't naturally talk about ourselves in third person, do we?

She thought about who she was, and who she wasn't. And realised she felt like Tiffany, but, younger? Yeah, maybe mid teenage. She asked inside and someone confirmed that was who she was and told her her name was Jade."

Tiff, was not having a good time...

"Hi, it's Tiff. This is day four of me being stuck in the front and Mia is unhappy with the lack of social mediaing. So I have to vent and she's gonna censor it afterwards. Basically so everyone can laugh at my pain and suffering more than they already are (and so we have a record of what's happening lol bc we aren't journaling like we should be! - Mia!).

So. Flaming Amber. She couldn't just leave it alone could she? This shouldn't have come out. We did nearly half a life not beeping knowing and it was blooping covert for a forking reason. I've been, it seems our predominant se*ual (did that really need censoring?!) alter and have done some things that apparently I'm feeling pooping shame for now for the first time I can remember. All my armour is coming off and I feel fracking vulnerable and just want this to be over. Seems I haven't actually felt hucking anything for 14 years. And have sabotaged some of the life while being essentially clucking void of feeling. How the boop do you process shame?! Amber says feel it. Mia says "just keep feeling just keep feeling". Flipping helpful.

So last night a teenage version of me showed up and is literally judging me. We have to resolve stuff but ugh. I've managed to upset the littles. I haven't spent much time with them and now I have to mucking entertain them when they're close and brotherbucking boop beep poop it's not fair just let me leave already!!!! Others switch in and within a couple of minutes are laughing as they feel themselves switch back to me!! Forking Isabel has bitched she "misses the old Tiffany". Mucksake it's not my fault I'm apparently feeling!!! I hope she has to go through this and it's hell. Others are now disagreeing with that sentiment because we are all suffering while individually sorting out our years of hidden crap!

I think that sums it up. Hopefully this will end soon and someone else can come out and be dorking miserable for a while. - Tiff.

Can I leave

By Tiff and Miya

I've been here long enough
I've decided I am actually Amber
This is all a delusion
~~We are~~
No
I am
Making this up
There aren't people
~~Laughing at me in my head~~
~~Nor am I aware~~
~~Of the face palming going on behind me~~
I've also had a full on crying want to break things event
CAN I LEAVE YET PLEASE

A conversation

Tiff and Jade

Tiff hey

Jade hi what are you doing oh ok interesting

T so I think we should talk

J um ok

T how are you feeling now?

J dumbstruck at what I became. Wtf happened to you me ugh. Ok I see.

T yeah apparently there are reasons

J I wonder who we might have been if he *(abusive ex in our twenties)* hadn't happened

T well we wouldn't have lost 6 years to him for one

J why don't you want to be loved?

T because it hurts.

J so it's better not to? Why did you have to sleep with so many people?

T escape? Prove I could? Prove I was worth something even if it was just sex

J isn't sex better in a loving relationship?

T I guess. I stopped feeling though. Just liked sex but no love

J but you don't want to do that now?

T no I don't know what I want tbh. I'm very confused. I feel unbalanced and like nothing is my choice. I want to have choices

J I always wanted love or maybe actually sex bc everyone else was doing it.

T It's all so confusing with the overlapping emotions and everyone feeling so different. I just fucking hate feeling vulnerable

J why?

T Because it's weak

J is it?! I don't think Amber is weak and she can be vulnerable?

T I guess

J what's going to happen to us? Will there always be two of us?

T I'm not sure tbh. We could fuse. Or stay separate. It's our choice. For now ig we spend time together and try to resolve whatever we can

Tiff was learning how much we get from the tap tapping. Let's go back to the book, just for another perspective...

"She and Tiff spent a bit of time together, with Tiff really struggling with the situation. Jade was unimpressed by the person she became. Didn't like Tiffany's attitudes to a lot of things, and was severely disappointed about a lot of future/historical behaviour. Even proclaiming "I don't really like Tiffany very much" at one point.

Tiffany was feeling judged (correctly), and began experiencing shame for the first time she could remember. She was struggling with that, with Jade in general, with having to be present and in the body all the time, and with the littles.

She was possibly the least maternal among them. It's not that she hated kids, she'd just prefer not to be around them. The littles picked up on this (that will happen when you share a brain, a consciousness, and a lot of memories) and were unhappy. They were used to getting some time out to play and do things but now they didn't feel welcome.

Mia tried helping Tiffany. Spending short amounts of time in the front, running her baths, making her coffees, even making her a cake (although Tiff felt like she did quite a bit of the cake)."

Day 6 of being default

By Tiff (and Stef and Mia)

I've been all over the place
Literally
This is bizarre

Spent time with teenage me (Jade)
Which was hard in the beginning
"I don't think I like Tiffany very much"
I kept fighting
Wanting this to be over
Avoiding the littles
Not doing any of the things we know are helpful
(other than the mandatory dog walk and yoga)
I gave up
I stopped fighting
Tried to "soften"
As they keep telling me to so
Kinda accepted that I'm here
When we were walking yesterday afternoon
I was chatting with Jade and we decided to try fusing
We're like um ok, what do we do?
Does this just happen?
Poof
Mia's in the front sending us back inside
About 10 minutes later we were back
Fused
I was 27 and Jade 15 ish
Together we were late teens
Last night was pretty rough
I've been a bit teary
Weird I remember school and it feels like it wasn't long ago I was there
(bleugh)
I keep seeing classrooms vividly
All I have been doing is trying to work out
What it is
I need to learn
Feel

Remember
To be able to leave
And let her get on with the life

Tiff and Jade, now one person, asked Mia if they could be older. They aged from late teens to late twenties with a quick visit inside. They considered their name, not being attached to either they already had. Interestingly, Cerys was one they considered (close to Caris). She felt different, changed, vulnerable, even signing off a status as: 'currently unnamed dramatically changed I'll never be the same again fml send help alter formerly known as Tiffany'. Although, others were getting restless...

"It Lolly I excaped I am older maybe 8 year old little Abby still my best friend ever tho!!!

Is this progress? She hasn't done this with me before. She's just messaged two friends to tell them she's older and then came here?! I'm like, what do I do?! Do I let her tell fb she's older? Inside are like yes!!! And I'm like um this looks crazy you know right? OH is this why the littles don't like me? And they're now saying you know you now look crazier than the new 8 year old, um no technically we're all the same person sooooo....

I'm still here. I guess I'm just Tiff bc I can't think of any other name (why does that cause a woohoo?) and I guess this is progress or at least change."

Tiger

By Stef

Day 8
'In the big brother house'
(Some joker)
Mia

She kept calling me
My Little Tiffany
(She is the perfect balance of sweet and annoying
If you hadn't noticed... Only one setting: lovely)

It was bothering me
I suddenly realised
Maybe I haven't
Only been here
Since we were 16
When I thought
My first memories were

Other alters
Have different versions
Of themselves
Often
They have a little
I asked
In the head
I heard
"I'm scared and I want love"

So
I found her
Tiger she chose
As her name
In 20 seconds
(I've been trying for days and can't)
I've been here
As long as everyone else
It's a lot to process

Hilarious
This child
I told her to stop
Putting her fingers in her mouth
So
She stuck her whole hand in
She's about 3
I guess I'm hanging out with the kids
Unfortunately
She keeps calling me mummy
I'm not a fan
The passive influence
Eating sweets I don't want
Is weird

I can't choose a name
Tiff
Tiffany
I'm not her anymore
I know who I am now
And I'm not Tiff
Mia
Accidentally called me Steph
That might work

And Tiger
A little bit hiding
Says 'hi' to the world
Watch out though
We're definitely some of the troublemakers

It was still a little more suffering before she was freed though. Amazingly, Amber was managing to work around Tiff's crisis. She could schedule clients,

Tiff would be in the body until an hour before the appointment and Amber would then be able to switch for more than a couple of minutes. Then she'd dog walk or shower to settle into the body, go and see her client, and immediately they would switch back as soon as she finished working.

"She has a client later so will be coming back at two to walk Jason and do that, and we know from the other day it is not good working when I'm around. She did a swap and had said she'd like me to receive the massage in return and subsequently I was around for a lot of the treatment she did and it was pretty awful lol.

I feel like something might be coming up... when other trauma sharing has happened it's felt similar to this. That Amber thinks it's ok for me to feel like this in the morning, potentially have a trauma share imminently, and she's gonna go work this afternoon just seems crazy but she's proved us wrong before so we'll just see what happens. I just hope I get through this at some point in the next decade now.

Gonna try Steph for a while. Feels the most natural. Don't really like it but I can't find a name that I like that feels right. Obv Mia and Berlou are now calling me Stiff. Lots of memories coming out. Think we all hated school lol. That's my vent for now. - Steph. (Yeah it feels ok, suggestions still welcome tho lol)"

Tyrant

By Miya

The tyrant is gone!
A big emotional event!
She can leave!
No longer
Prisoner
Never coming back
Can't stay away
But

She is now
A cold
Hard
Bitch
Because she wants to be
Not because
That's how life made her

PHEW! I thought Stef's nonsense was going to last forever! I'm not even sure what the big emotional event was... Maybe she knows and isn't telling, it doesn't seem to have been written about though. Of course, the chief was back:

> "Normal service is resumed and you can expect to hear a lot more from myself and my entourage now Amber's back in charge and I can do whatever I want again (blah blah within reason blah blah)
>
> Stiff seems ok. Apparently she's returned to being a cold hard beach bc she wants to be one, not because that's how life made her! (She is super soft about Tiger though! Tiger won't leave her alone!) Amber did her treatment good. The body is a bit messy from all Stiff's stuff and Amber says don't get complacent bc she's sure someone else will need to process in the body soon enough!! Nooooooo!!! Nooo more trauma! Anyway, it's Lego time! From your favrit Mia Alex! Oh and others!"

Netball, flower arranging, music: slow progress

Spotify

By Amber

My liked songs
Have been destroyed
By the children
In my head

They kept on swimming/feeling, and Berlou was getting more ambitious in things she wanted to do. Amber had a client who mentioned she wanted to go to a ladies Back to Netball thing at a local school. Netball is like basketball but you can't move with the ball and is more a sport girls play in school; that, and dodge ball are the only enjoyable things we remember from PE, and Berlou wanted to revisit it. An older version of Berlou (AL) once expressed interest too, so it wasn't surprising.

Amber got in touch with them and explained our situation, and Isabel volunteered to take Berlou (Amber did not want to go!) They booked it, and on the day:

> "I'm going to do a thing like a real person and I've been wondering all day why I'm not anxious but now we're about to go I found it! Argh! Why would I want to do this?! People?! I can barely speak. I've aged to about

20 maybe a bit older. Now I have to go and do things! I don't even have a proper name damn it! Berlou?! I can't say Amber bc if someone calls me Amber it will trigger Amber out - argh! Ok. Isabel and Amber are coming with me. Wish me luck pls! And just in case you forgot a few months ago I was like 4 and cried all the time! This is actually huge! ARGH! Ok thanks I'm done! - Berlou."

It was, in Berlous's words, a medium success. She got there, started to speak to people and panicked. Isabel took over, got her inside and told people to call her Berlou. Isabel and Berlou were blended and it was going on, they'd enjoyed the warm up, and had played a game one direction, then..

"We switched positions and we were goal defense so were meant to be trying to stop this goal attacker scoring and oh my goodness she was really good and I think I must've got scared and ran away inside because Isabel was thrown out clueless, she hadn't watched the couple of YouTube videos with me in the morning, had no idea what she was doing, and kept swearing a lot!! At one point she was muttering away to herself "I'm going to kill the people in my head" and someone heard her and asked what she said!! The body is unsurprisingly broken today. Haven't seen Isabel today to thank her, last night she came back out for 20 seconds just to complain about how awful it was! And that Stef can take me next time if I want to go again! - Berlou"

They laughed about Isabel's fun for days! And Berlou wanted to go again, but, as per usual, things beyond their control kept happening and it's now three months later and we haven't been back, you never know though.

With Berlou being proactive about her ageing and healing, it was affecting Mia as well, as they were still 'conjoined twins' - oh, about that, the connection was at the hip - Mia's left and Berlou's right - and they can still feel where they were joined! (Nothing was surprising anymore, obviously).

Mia had aged, was back to teenage and 'unbearable' she spoke to Granma...

"So granma said if I'm happy being little I should be little so me and Berlou disconnected ourselfs and I came back to 7! We were fused for a day bc I was confused and thought by being little I can't be important but we had a big meeting and Amber given me lots of responsibility! Berlou and Alex are staying together (me and Alex were fused and then all three of us fused and then I split from them two and they stayed together!) So I now have my subsystem back! I forgot I can't access them properly when I'm fused with people! So I found Mia 21 so she's happy she can be out and about again!"

Oh yeah, I remember this. Mia put Berlou through a rough day, not knowing what she wanted, generally being a pain! But, as per most really weird things though, it worked out, and Mia essentially handed Alex over to Berlou. The three of them were fused for a day, and when they separated Alex stayed with Berlou. Berlou and Alex are still together.

Mia did a littles check in:

"Lolly and Tiger (both extroverts definitely and love orange!)
Jasmine and Sophie (Sophie was Tilly she finally choose a name she happy wiff!)
Carabel (little Cara and Anabel fusion) and Abigail (Abigail lived inside with Kai and Cherry for a while but she's joined the gang and hangs around wiff Carabel!)"

And Amber started examining some of Mia's behaviours, which Mia did not appreciate...

"I get a bit obsessive. Apparently Lego is an obsession and 1000+ hours on animal crossing last year demonstrates this too. And Amber did some thinking and says it's a recognisable consistent behaviour that needs to be addressed but it's ok for now we notice and I try not to nag (I did some nagging last week and got in trouble A LOT!!)"

That behaviour? Same one that means that there are different versions of the same person, fighting over this book, pouring every last drop of energy into it, ignoring everything else. We're ambitious. We like a challenge, we like to prove people wrong, and we like to do things well. I hope that shows. Yeah, we're a bit crazy, but Amber wouldn't have achieved anything without us. (I can feel eye-rolling behind me). And Mia came up with a new catchphrase.

> "We are trying to be mindful and I say we have to stop killing time and start filling time! So I'm going to make a great big chocolate cake and eat it all! Oh we are so achy after Isabel and Berlou went to netball! Things hurt that we didn't know exist!! From Mia OG 7yo Chief Little and second in command!"

Slowly, they were exploring being social, as a we. And were introducing more people to the world of dissociative disorders! One of the earlier people Amber told about what was going on, was her friend Vikki. Vikki had been amazing, balancing curiosity and concern and making everyone feel comfortable enough to talk to her. They went to a flower arranging morning with her, while the other people there made a little posy pot each - the gang of children in a thirty eight year old body felt free and went a little bit crazy! Jasmine had made a beautiful posy pot, but it didn't last long...

> "the littles got all confident and kept diving out and adding more flowers to our already excessive posy pot!! Tiger was on a mission and was v funny! And we aren't sure who but someone popped out, looked at the flowers we'd assembled and said "that's lovely!" ... the woman next to us said "um you made it?" Whoever it was just said "no I didn't we got DID Jasmine made it"!! It was so full we got home and rearranged them again into two! Tiger and Lolly's is the orange one and Jasmine did the other again!"

The peace didn't last long though, and Jasmine's presence propelled her into the healing hotspot.

"Blah blah blah. We're back at it. I'm Jasmine +20 odd years. Always been here. If we didn't know what we know I would think I'm just Amber in a really bad mood. So I didn't grow up to be a Disney princess then. Nope just part of a 38 yo huck up with some serious mental health problems.

Tried to cancel yoga twice and wasn't allowed and they made me go, turned out that that was ok. Looking at what everyone else has been through (specifically Stef and her 9 day front stuck healing event lol - I am not doing that crap!)

So I know that I'll need to process whatever the hell I've been storing in the body physically for the last nearly 4 decades. Last night when I appeared there was a LOT of pain around the hips and lower back so I'm guessing that's all mine. Gonna try to do things and not fight like Stef did. As per a lot of people my first focus is what the hell my name will be. Jasmine is still with the littles, I don't really like Jas, Mia keeps calling me OJ (old jasmine lol). I dunno. Jada is nice? People keep saying Yasmin but that surely just makes everyone think of bloody Baywatch? Although that was a while ago I think right? What even is time? Why am I not a Disney princess? Wtaf is this chaos? Who can be arsed? Who even has time for this crap, oh right, we do. Oh great, here comes Mia to answer my questions.

Jada is nice? Yes it is we like it!
People keep saying Yasmin but that surely just makes everyone think of bloody Baywatch? Um ok
Although that was a while ago I think right? I dunno
What even is time? I'm not sure but it's v weird!
Why am I not a Disney princess? I don't think that was ever going to happen even if we not crazy tbh OJ. Wtaf is this chaos? DID/OSDD. We'll maybe get diagnosed in the next decade if we lucky.
Who can be arsed? We don't haff much choice.

Awesome. That's cleared everything up nicely then. - OJ Wait that's worse it's just either orange juice or some guy that got away with murder?! Jas."

She just stayed Jas.

"Me (Jas): "what if this isn't real? Some kinda computer game? Are we dead?" Mia: "ooh depersonalisation no one's been here for a while!"

Also this morning "ok what if I'm Amber? What if I'm actually crazy and this is some kinda psychosis?" Also, Mia: "you aren't Amber, go to yoga" gotta say the support from this head is lacking sometimes. Amber is kinda available but not. She said hi to Sara at yoga anyway. It feels like she's just leaving me to work this out by myself. Which looking at everything else that's happened seems that's what we need to do individually.

I'm making progress. Fused with Jas, the teenage one (was fused with the other two teens and then split sometime recently apparently, guess they realised they needed to sort their stuff out individually). I was teenage for a day, which as per everyone else, was horrible. Asked to be older last night and literally after crying in yoga and chatting to Sara suddenly that happened. Dunno maybe late twenties/early thirties. I'm miserable. Jasmine was inexplicably sad so I guess I'm depression personified? I can kinda laugh about it most of the time tho but pretty down this morning.

We realised Sophie holds fear. No one has been scared of anything really, so now there's a lot of fear floating around.

I was told that you should never share trauma between alters… lol. So we're definitely doing this wrong. But looks like this conv happened before and the outcome was wth else do we do when it's all happening. Amber somehow got us in this situation where we are all individually healing. Taking turns in the body to process. It's insane. And we have the space and time to do this leisurely? That's impressive forward thinking/luck, I've gotta say. She has a client tomorrow. So that's good, hopefully I can be done and go back to the shadows ASAP lol. Apologies for the overshare. Seems this is where we're logging what's happening, opposed to like a journal or something more sensible. - Jas."

Jas found Soph, an older version of Sophie, which made things easier for her. There was no big climactic event to Jas's front stuckness, they just kept going, Amber seeing more clients as they found her. And Mia kept being Mia, of course.

"Effryone happy (except I'm not allowed to sort out the old Lego today and maybe cried at granma and said I never allowed and made Amber look mean but she really said I allowed to do it any time but now!!) it good having Amber around. Me and Berlou and littles keep getting distracted which is why Amber say she allow almost whole day to clean bc she know what we like! from Mia! Hope ur all having good days and weeks!!"

Amber had learnt that everything took a lot longer than it should do. Trying to clean and tidy a room? We're guaranteed to get distracted by things a lot, and it will subsequently take at least four times as long as it should. And Mia got funnier.

"Just contemplating adding to Amber's boring old Mia less Instagram bio "My other selves are less boring" and linking to us. Then maybe "They're also hilarious too, and I love Mia more than life itself". I can feel the eyes. I mean she isn't exactly saying no. Although I'm starting to worry about my safety. Send help. She might be homicidal."

Mia didn't add it to Amber's Instagram! I believe her own currently reads "Amber's more interesting other selves", though. And if you ever suggest to Mia that she might be Amber, she'll probably tell you no way, that she's "not that boring".

They were learning all the time about trauma processing. Mostly just by figuring it out by themselves, but fortunately Amber had been gathering the tools she needed to get through this, for years. Music was one method they used for trauma processing and has been a constant. I'll let Mia tell you about it.

> "Someone will fixate on a song and repeat the poop out of it until the emotions that are related to it somehow subside... it's an old behaviour pattern that we've done a lot before even knowing we were a we. Like when Ray died we did one song for weeks, crazy lol. So mostly they're nice gentle songs... the ones that you can feel in your heart... wanna feel sad and lonely, we got you lol 'Oh Wonder' by Lonely Star, that was one of Berlou's (she's actually our resident DJ!). Anyway. I won't bore you with a list of our songs and get to the point. Jas has looked at this behaviour and is like ok what's my song? It doesn't really seem to work like that though, like wands, the song chooses the wizard! But anyway. She decided she's chosen her song. So for the last few days we've mostly been listening to The Passenger by Iggy Pop in the head. She is majorly hung up on that this isn't her life, she is "just a passenger". Funny, a bit sad, quite insightful. - Mia"

Ah yes, Berlou being the resident DJ! Some of us are definitely more musically focused than others, and some of us always have music playing. Berlou (and another version of her), usually has music playing. It gets louder as they get closer, and quieter as they go deeper. Amber's been known to shout "shut more doors" into the head, when we can hear music playing. Another time they were sat watching TV and kept hearing snippets of Braveheart, mostly the music, but bits of dialogue too. Assume someone was watching Braveheart inside - it's one of the films we've seen enough times that it's possibly possible. We think a lot of what we watch and read gets recreated inside. We recently rewatched Downton Abbey, along with hearing Carson and Mary Crawley in the head at times, another odd thing that happened was Amber found herself looking up the floorplan of Highclere Castle (where Downton is filmed). We assume an internal architect wanted that information...

Berlou mentioned when Ray died, so I'm just going to squeeze something in here about that. Amber wrote a blog post, Ray Dog Grief. I went through it, mostly just grief and dogs, obv. This was interesting though:

> "Since losing Ray, I've struggled with working. Both trying to find clients and the actual treatments themselves, at times. To practice myofascial release, you need to switch off your brain and fully tune in to the client and their body. The first few weeks were really tough, I tried to still my mind, focus on my hands and heart, but I couldn't shift out of my own grief, I'd just hear *"I can't do this, I just want to cry"*. It's getting easier. I've still not been proactive in finding clients, but these last couple of weeks, they've been finding me and I've been doing some good treatments."

Is that how everyone describes their own thoughts? Well, it makes sense knowing what we know now. And, she had learnt that what we've been seeing was necessary for any of this to be healed...

> "There has been lots of learning through this time. The biggest being that you have to be patient and can't rush grief. Somewhere around week 3 after Ray's death I decided I should just 'get over it'. I stopped crying and tried not to think about Ray and his death, but that led to some horrible depression type feelings and a lot of beating myself up and anxiety. Allowing myself to feel the pain and let it out through talking and crying about my loss was much better than a self-hatred whirlpool of misdirected pain. At the moment I'm still often sad, and that's ok, at times I've been really worried it will spiral into full blown depression, and sometimes it has felt that way. But this isn't depression, it's grief. I almost got sucked back into depression though by avoiding my true feelings. You've got to feel it to heal it."

Peach Plus

Mid September, and they were still coming. Peach appeared one morning.

> "We got newbies! Had another turn up who didn't know who she was, first time in a while someone had to take the stairs one at a time laughing so much bc they have little legs even though they got big legs!! Did some investigating and her favourite colour is peachy pink so she choose the name Peach! She thought Peaches but Amber said we can't all be named after Geldoff children (although there's only Tiger but whatever!!)
>
> So anyway we got coffee and Peach was suddenly old! She so much like Amber that granma thought she was Amber! So nice and so much positivity! We think she fused with Amber now but Peach still there and Jacob came out again, he a little that said hi the other day but people were busy at the time! We think he maybe got an older self too!
>
> Very busy and switchy today, everyone popping through and feeling the new energy, exciting times! From Mia!"

Peach is quite wonderful, loves music, and 'bounces on the hips', all the time. Even bounced out of the mental nurse's office a couple of months ago, with him shouting "Be careful going down those stairs!" as she left! Yeah, this optimism? Excitement at newcomers? It didn't last, obviously.

> "Feeling pretty awful, wrote a depressing poem instead of getting dressed. Lola said hi finally and has joined us, Lolly's older self. She'd been waiting for the right time but that's unlikely to happen. I'm, I guess,

Peaches. Older Peach who got here yesterday. Gotta say, we love the way all these adults have to work with names their child versions are choosing first. Can we all really have two or three (more?) versions of ourselves? Everyone except Amber anyway. Already any enthusiasm I came out carrying has been depleted."

Fragments

By Peaches, Jas and Lola

How many more ways can one person hurt
Divided and fragmented
The parts they hold
The deepest anxieties
Precious like trophies
Unwilling to share
Hurting and scared
We did not ask for this
We do not want to be known
We want to keep our secrets

It's not even trauma
They think we should know
Why we hurt
But we hide it from ourselves too
Boxed and hidden
Do not disturb
Do not open
But it keeps happening
Peeling and peeling
Layer after layer
Pain after pain

How much can the body take

It cries for rest but we let it not
It needs respite and time to heal
It needs to be seen
Acknowledged and honoured
My pain I feel in the body

Anxiety

It courses through its veins
Playing its soulful song
Familiar yet alien
An uninvited guest
Always present
Always reminding
What it wants
The need for connection
To be seen
To be alone
To be validated
To hide
To scream
To die

I know I spoke about music and trauma processing somewhere, but another fun thing about music is it's a very powerful switch. We all like certain different songs and genres, and especially when there has been a processing attachment, it's something they can't fight. Mia managed to accidentally exploit this one day...

"I managed to arrange yesterday to trigger myself out today by accident!!!

The miseries have had their feets right under the table all morning. Then they went to shower and queued some miserable songs on Spotify and

I'd already got my party tunes queued yesterday! They're there wallowing in their misery and suddenly there's a crab rave of littles happening in the bathroom!!!!

Me and Berlou are staying. Not sure what's happening with Amber bc Peaches keeps thinking she is Amber but we aren't sure... they thought about fusing... no I don't think they're together. Guess the miseries need to process their misery but rn we have to go shop. Shouting for Amber isn't working. I'll find Isabel. And have permanent positive music triggers until we're done shopping and they can do their crying or whatever! Ooh yeah DID is FUN (jk) - Mia, Berlou, the miseries, the littles, and a moody Isabel!!"

And, later that day... (Still the same day, since the awful poem, gotta credit the Peach family - they are processing FAST)...

"This is absolute bullshit. We aren't "processing" or healing. These are just all the feelings that have always been here that incapacitate us. Fucking Mia before was like "Oh, this is depression!" like yeah no shit. We don't want to eat or do anything. Can't sleep. Not allowed to smoke the one thing that helps. "NOT ALLOWED".

We're still Lola, Jas, Soph and Sasha (was Peaches, rebranded already). It's weird as you start writing the consciousness changes. Mia's more present and I guess Jessica. So yeah this is depression. Dreaming about death. Every fucking cell being simultaneously burnt and frozen. Unable to move forwards. Being dragged backwards. Oh ffs, we remembered the ex that died. That was a blow. Poor guy. Like there's so much physical emotion in the body but we have no idea whose. It feels wrong that we could all process whateverthefuck without even knowing what it's attached to? Actually there maybe is more happening just below the surface than we realise. Looking back at everyone else's healing events, Stef didn't have to know what she was feeling and she seems ok now.

Really? We can just feel bad and "let it go"?! We're not buying it. Mia's a pest. Like we can't even be miserable in peace. What even is the point.

Why are we even bothering sharing, like anyone would give a crap or would read this absolute whining bullshit. Mia says go for it and apparently sharing how we feel can help and also she wants a record for the book, yeah that'll be a really great read: woman who struggles with mental health problems for almost 40 years finds out they aren't actually her problems and it's all the other people unwittingly sharing a brain with her that made her feel shit most of the time, finds them and makes them feel their feelings so she can feel better. Awesome, Mia's curious about how angry we are. Amber told her to let us do what we need to do. Thanks for the help and support. Just get on with it, cry, wallow, don't eat, dream about not existing. Blah. Ok I'm done for now. - Sasha (maybe, peaches wasn't working anyway, and tbf at this point like anyone outside of the head even cares what our names are, we all just keep fucking coming with our repetitive bullshit and never ending weirdness claiming to be different people. Lol.)

Ooh, yay! They wrote a synopsis for me!! That will come in handy later and save loads of time. Anyway, they suffered for another couple of days. Amber was trying to restrict the cannabis use though and this was annoying them; they hit upon the idea of negotiating productivity for green, logical and impressive. They were stuck in the front, bored, going through the motions, not allowed to do what most teenagers at some point want to do - lie on the sofa watching trash TV with a smoke.

So they started going through Amber's work emails and messages. Found all the people that had been ignored or got a "I'll let you know when I'm working again" type response - remembering odd messages from as far back as December 2020. They sent a ton of emails. Did the work, I guess Amber would come closer at times and tell them what to write, or they just accessed what they needed to know. They scheduled phone calls with new and old clients for Amber to take, seriously, looking back at this, I'm super impressed. They literally did it all, then they're like "Ok, you've got three clients this week and two next week because of us, CAN WE SMOKE NOW PLEASE?" Obviously, they got their green.

And now, everyone forgets Penelope exists and Mia and Amber get VERY confused. They also ran over a squirrel and got bitten to pieces taking it to the vets to die faster. That was rough, oh and then spent days trying to get a tetanus jab, because of the damn dead squirrel. And:

> "I AM AMBER! Ok well I'm not anymore, but we realised that I'm her little that's why she no got a little! But I kicked Maya out and became me and did all this year etc so now not Amber but explains why I'm so strong and always here! Berlou made the point that it *might* have been part of the plan (if someone somewhere does have a plan. Someone knows more than us anyway lol)... so if I hadn't split from Maya we might have noticed sooner, we might have aged, I might have not been so set in my little ways. but then I wouldn't have been here like I am to fuse with Berlou and everyone else I helped heal! So to conclude: I'm Amber. Staging a coup. Oh damn no we have to go work she can be boss still for now from Miamber I JOKING !!! MIA"

She isn't Amber. This is hilarious. Amnesia ftw. Ugh, I just read ahead and we're about to see Mia see me for the first time, so frustrating.

> "We been back trauma processing again today, we just do it for fun now. Been thinking more about work. It's funny. Trauma processing isn't what you think so often. It can be subtle. Easy to turn away from. We've been thinking a bit how it feels counter productive: walking into pain, poking it, seeing where it goes, how deep it is, (hi Jessica!) I feel seen and not comfortable. No one's called me out like that before. See ya, good luck Mia. oh damn she gone! We were saying good things! Effryone in hysterics. Um so yes, trauma processing weird. Can be done anytime anything anywhere. U can no what it's about or not no. U can be REALWY in the body or eyes glazed over no one home away wiff the fairies. I bored now writing wiff out Jessica, this is Mia signing off over and out Mia ramblings complete (4 now)"

See what I mean about the language? And Lolly was around a bit, more charity shop trips happened, yoga, dog walks, the kids played with stickers and lego, etc., kinda boring? Doubt it will be for long.

Too much

By Lolly and Miya

I make dis
He called George
She says I can post it
I say do I not post too much
She say no it ok
U do what u want
I proud off u

Too cute, as is Mia.

Pest

By Mia

Why do I front all the time?
Am I technically the host?
I kind of am the host

The big boss meanie
She says
You aren't technically the host
You're just a pest who won't stay away

If I could go for a walk with Jason
And slam the door leafing her here
I wud
I just need to perfect my cloning machine

So, everything seems to be ok ish, nothing major, let's go crazy and have a sound bath and reiki on consecutive days. Amber can tell you about it.

"Amazing sound bath last night as per usual with Sara. Last time I was there we had just started on our journey learning about our multiplicity. Isabel and I were communicating but we were still unaware of the others, and what DID was. Now though we've spent almost a year trying to work this chaos out, trauma processing is second nature (well, it is, for everyone, always - this is just complex as we are many sharing one body with decades of unresolved trauma).

We already knew that trauma was stored in the body, now we've had the unfortunate opportunity to observe the body from many different perspectives. It's a different experience for us all, and we all keep all of our baggage in it somewhere.

As we lay down I was so much more aware of the buzzing around my body, just a little layer of anxiety, Maya was close by and has been through huge healing events but being around people still makes her a bit nervous.

Sara's singing was entrancing, some nice tingly sensations, the drum managed to quiet my ridiculous monkey brain for a few minutes (it's impossible to shut everyone up at once). So much was happening physically while we're lying there, some of us trying to stay present focusing on the body, others not so engaged.

Often we don't even have to know what we are feeling, but (in Mia's words) the important thing is to "just keep feeling, just keep feeling" (Dory style pls thx - Mia). So it was a good hour of being with the body, away from the phone (other than about three quarters way through madam appears "ugh this is soooooo boring. I need to check my socials. Can I check my phone? Under the blanket? Purwease?" "No. Inside. Now")"

I'm loving Amber's openness and honesty here. It can't be easy to say out loud "This is me, this is us". Interesting, she and Mia had a conversation about this recently, they feel it works well because they both get to hide behind each other? Amber is mostly always present at the moment, at least keeping an eye, but giving everyone the freedom to do what they want. The Mia/Penelope energy is free to get carried away, writing a book, dreaming of a better future, oh, sorry, where were we? Amber?

"Usual but slightly later bedtime routine. Got to bed and we're just buzzing. There was so much activity it was crazy. Physically and mentally, it's a shame we can't get actual words written in the headspace because we thought a lot of words last night.

Awake before 5 and got up. Mia was in the front. "Oh great, here we go again". Such a strange release though, often we are aware of just how physical trauma releasing is, we do a lot in yoga and walking too, unwinding, shaking and crying are common if stuff comes up at home. This was definitely much more energetic and spanned wider. Started around the pelvis and there was a lot of physical sensations and shaking, and it moved slowly over just a few minutes up the physical body and out through the head. God knows what that one was, Mia asked and it was related to Peach/Sasha we think.

Interestingly I had a reflexology session booked with Eve today, got there and learnt she does reiki now too, so asked for reiki instead. We'd done some releasing physically in yoga this morning but I had been thinking I should find some energetic assistance soon. Kinda reassuring to have someone else tell me how much activity there is going on, she even said she'd never felt such energy come off someone's head, yup it seems many consciousnesses in one head will have that effect... we've played with energy before with a lot of us present and it can be practically magnetic, there's power in numbers it seems even if they all share a body.

> The last year has been the biggest event of my life, we're still processing. But I'm (personally) more stable than I've ever been, from the outside we look like a mess because we are, but I know who is feeling what though now and can manage it, and am finally working again (with a new internal apprentice, believe it or not, Berlou is desperate for us to drive my practice towards trauma healing). Many of our alters have been through their own journeys - Stef's was a nine day event involving losing 14 years of emotional armour, being judged by her 15 year old self, becoming one with her 15 year old self, and finally finding her child self and (reluctantly) becoming mummy to her. I couldn't make this up."

Agreed. And yay, they're about to be disproved on the Miamber relationship they'd weirdly made up a couple of weeks ago. We can only assume Pen was stuck or working somewhere and got shaken out with the sound bath and reiki, but we don't know.

> "We were wrong. We found Pen again. I'm her little. Berlou is a split from Amber like Alex, why they're happy together. Maya is Amber's trauma holder. We were so confused because Maya and I first came through together as Amber and Penelope have lived their life together. Pen was created very early we believe... ugh it's so confusing... but there was an internal alter formed at the time of the first trauma who managed everything. We think she made Pen to help Amber. I dunno. I just needed to expel this from my head and thought I'd demonstrate just how much we have no fucking clue what's going on and will change our minds next week. Ooh, maybe find out Amber's making us all up? YES PLEASE - Mia but a bit older hence fucks. Aw crap wait what am I Pen? Fml. Dissociation SUCKS. Ok I am Pen now, Mia just randomly slid up as she does then we got confused and now we're both here. Has anyone said 'poor Amber' lately? (Lol, the laughter inside, bitches)."

Yeah, Amber's fine. We still don't have clarity on any of this. Like this is the only time I've seen them say specifically Maya is Amber's trauma holder? I don't know, surely she's Pen's - Mia and Maya came through together. See, no idea.

We guess a lot of things, often just have to let them be and accept we might never understand anything.

So, Penelope was back, again. After some digging around she worked out that she'd been AWOL for about three months, with so little contact that she was completely forgotten about! When she was searching though, she actually found that three days before her return Mia had gone to the brief introduction she had written on Instagram and commented, "Where r u Penelope?', and someone had commented back "I'm still here Mia, it's ok, I'll be back soon".

Pen had a lot to catch up on, there had been new alters, huge progress with Berlou and Maya, a brand new Stef, and the ongoing debate over the depression/mania the Penelope family suffered from.

> "I'm definitely bringing baggage with me, there's been speculation previously about me and my depression/possible mania… I hope I don't cause too much disruption (inside are like it's fine, if it's not you it'll be someone else!) Trying to not be overwhelmed by everything but it's not easy, glad today's tasks are just clean for clients Amber has here over the next couple of days. Still amazed at how quickly everyone forgot about me - Pen"

Sadly, Pen had her turn coming, and it wasn't nice. She seemed to be suffering from the world's worst hangover, and yet they hadn't had a drink for months. A relentless thirst that wouldn't go away, shaking/vibrating, uncomfortable digestive system, it was unpleasant, we assumed this was possibly a long overdue hangover - Penelope is definitely a stoner, and we think she probably likes a drink too. She and Amber kept being confused about who was who, and Pen's catchphrase became "Crap, I thought I was Amber", for a little while.

Working was getting interesting for Amber too, now that they had good communication and others were taking an interest in myofascial release and the trauma-releasing aspects of it. Mia can tell you…

"So Amber had client. Everything going well then she's working on their abdomen and Berlou pipes up "there's sadness there. Tell her it will get better". Ambers like oh ffs I can't do this! Last time when she got "messages" while working she'd thought it was intuition or a higher self or whatever. Anyway Berlou was like "just tell her, it's just because I'm telling you that you're being weird". So Amber mentions the sadness. Then B is like "yeah she's scared too, tell her it will be ok and she doesn't need to be scared anymore". Ugh Amber can hear me and is interfering. She says that everyone is sad and scared at times, it's not surprising. Whatever. Anyway they loved the session and will be telling their friends about Amber and afterwards spoke of the sadness and fear so whatever, Berlou helped. - Mia"

Caris

Scars

By Caris

Scars
Can still
Hurt years
After you think
They've healed

They had a nice little break from the old TP, spent some time with their parents at home and had a little Scotland jolly. They hadn't been back home for long before the familiar anxiety filled process began again. They'd noticed Cara and Isabel kept signing things together, and their little counterparts had been fused for a while happily. Cara balanced Isabel; this had been observed, and it seemed the trauma sharing had been those two getting together. It wasn't a surprise, and it was a welcome progress.

My Carisabel

By Mia

We've all
Been on a journey
But my Isabel
She was the first
To make the jump

The bravest
She knew
She would forget everything
Have to piece together
The puzzle
With Amber
It was hard
But they fought
To communicate
To share
To help each other
After months
Working through trauma alone
I came
Then others
We realised
Isabel
Hadn't been
Just Isabel
But
A kind of
Trojan horse
Others had been processing
Through her
As the reveal progressed
She did her job
She protected
She fell in love
With me
(Easy)
One day
She'd healed
Softened enough

To be able to
Share a space
With another
She and Cara
Fused
Days of anxiety
Trauma sharing
We all suffered
While they worked
But it was worth it
Carisabel
Caris
Is a new person
She's still strong
Will fight
To the death
But
She's calmer
The hyper
Vigilance
Unneeded now
She can laugh
And smile
It's a beautiful thing
She's a beautiful thing
She cries
Oh wow
There's a first time
For everything

Isabel rarely, if ever, smiled or laughed (a lifetime of pain, fear and frustration management will do that), and in therapy that week Caris did most of it. She was, quite literally, a different person, laughing and smiling, it was a joy for everyone to see and feel. She took great pleasure in telling their therapist that it was huge healing (he agreed) and they were doing amazingly (he agreed).

"It's Caris. Whenever we've talked about final fusion, becoming one, it's always been me, Isabel, who categorically stated I did not want to fuse. I wanted to stay being me. I wanted to stay being angry. More often than not, we don't know what we are feeling, we feel more physically and energetically than mentally. Although, we so often forget whatever we've just been thinking about that perhaps we do - wait, can amnesia be about your own thoughts too? Because we have the whole "we don't have noticeable amnesia thing going on but if we widen it to include thoughts we 100% have amnesia" thing. Well, that's not how I thought this was going to go.

Anyway. Cara and I fused. Amber checked in with her yesterday morning (when we're fused our original selves/energies can still be "tuned in to", oh and we've been thinking a lot recently about consciousness as energetic, when we come back into the body it feels like we do actually come back into the body) she asked how Cara was and just got a big grin and "feeling strong" in response. We're still learning who we are, obviously. It's feasible we're splits from each other, and assume it's been that way since we were young.

Since the system reveal I've (Is) been limited in my fronting time due to my instability and anger. While it's easier for Amber now that she can genuinely say "I'm sorry, that wasn't me, it won't happen again", and is relieved to know she wasn't actually responsible for a lot of the things Stef and I have done, it's still hard, it's her body and her life (eek - I'm being shouted at, no it's our body our life. Blah blah two Ambers - one the whole and one Amber the alter who lived most of the life.)

So to sum up, it's still early days of our surprise fusion, inside are laughing at me thinking it was a surprise lol, but this could be really good for us. I hope I can start contributing to the system instead of hindering it. Cara is a beautiful soul, I'm– aw she's telling me not to gush. But this is good. I'm going back to bed. - Caris (and likely Jessica? Affirmative lol ooh she's all prickly - what do you want, to be seen or not seen? She says she's not talking about this on a Facebook post)."

Yeah, I don't like it! Let me do my job!

Faith, Astrid, and Jacob

Care Bear

By unknown and Miya

Not sure who I am
Might know in a minute
Just lying
Eyes open
Care bear in front of me
Eyes close
Eyes open
No care bear?
I'm cuddling the care bear
Of course
Nope, still don't know

I'm guessing we'll never know who wrote that.

We're into November 2021 now, they managed some social interactions occasionally, although sometimes things can go wrong... One day, they go for a coffee with a friend, Amber orders a soy latte. Peach pops out, asks if the pumpkin spice is vegan... Amber comes back "she's going to ruin my coffee, isn't she?"... obviously the two women behind the counter glare at Amber, one of them says "I'm not making yours yet"... Amber's trying to recover, trying to explain the perfectly normal and logical situation that a child inside her own head ordered the pumpkin spice and Amber was referring to her, not the people making coffee... Not sure if it would have been just the pumpkin spice flavour in the coffee, but Peach enjoyed it.

There were still more little people making themselves known. Faith and Astrid joined the collective. Faith was found when Amber was unwinding one day, she realised that her arm and hand weren't hers, put her right hand (that she was controlling), into her left, it squeezed, she squeezed it back, and out popped Faith. Astrid was teeny tiny, and another that giggled, taking one step at a time down stairs, with her little legs in a big body.

Mia was struggling though.

Apocalypse

By Mia

I am so lonely
Life is basically poo
Always will be

No one likes us
Cause we are weird
I want friends
But scared

They just think
I'm weird
Or vaguely interesting

I miss
When we were
Just Amber

I ruined it all

It was better
When we just
Had depression
And anxiety

I hope
For the apocalypse
Now
Because
I'm not allowed
To kill myself

Cookie

By Mia

That feeling
When u
Feel so rubbish
U can't even
Eat a cookie
That's pretty poo

She always bounces back, but Mia was tiring for sure. The littles were getting braver though...

"Hello! It lolly and tiger and peach! So Mia was all miserable and we went to yoga and we were very excited bc it was Koreen hatha and she not done a Monday morning for ages and we went and then it was meant to be just us and one other but she didn't come! So Koreen said to amber what would u like to do? Hatha yin or we could talk? And amber said well I'd like to get my children out and let them do hatha with u if that's ok? So we all got to do yoga!!! Us and Jacob and Sophie and faith and jasmine and Abigail all did a bit and it was such fun because we were allowed to be ourselfs! Hot yoga Commonside is the best we love it so much! We are going to try to do things now and we haff a nice walk in a bit wiff a frend! Mia still sad but we try cheer her up! Hope u all haff good days! From lolly tiger and peach!"

I'll grab Amber's version of events, she wrote about it too.

"Things are settling here with us, maybe, we hope, lol. This morning I went to yoga, Mia was upset and being difficult but we got there. Amazingly it ended up being a 1:1 when the other person who had booked didn't show up, it was with Koreen so she asked what I would like to do... well... I asked if I could let the children in my head do some yoga with her! They had such fun being able to interact and giggle, wobble, fall over and just generally be our very strange selves.
When we got home, a few of them wanted to write a review, so one of our older selves helped them as the language would be very strange otherwise... I couldn't bring myself to let them use it and tag HYC, but I want to share their review here (and they are over the moon that I am - being seen and validated is very important to many of us, even the young ones).

This is Lolly, Tiger and Peach's review of Hot Yoga Commonside!

'We have been going to Hot Yoga Commonside for a very long time, over 7 years! We love it so much, we love how the heat makes it feel like a mini holiday, we love how amazing all the teachers are, and we love how welcome they always make us feel. We are children in a DID system (many people, one body, caused by childhood trauma). Today we had a lot going on just beneath the surface (we spend a lot of time processing old and new trauma atm), anyway we went to yoga and it was just us! Koreen was so nice, she asked what we would like to do and because we don't get to spend much time out in the real world interacting, our host asked Koreen if we could do yoga with her. Koreen said yes so we were all allowed to be ourselves! We had so much fun and we love how yoga is fun to do and so good for the body! We don't think we would have healed nearly as much as we have in the last year without having the support of the Hot Yoga Commonside community and the physical benefits of yoga. It is the best place! We love it, thank you Koreen and everyone there! (Grown ups helped us write this as the language would have been even worse if we had!) from Lolly and Tiger and Peach'."

Amber didn't know what to do with this review, Lolly, et al., had been brave enough to be themselves through a yoga class, and then wanted to write about it. She pondered sending it to the yoga studio but decided that would be a bit too weird for them to use anywhere, so, put herself out there again and shared it from her own Facebook profile. The other thing that happened during the class was Mia popping out, looking around, huffing, saying "Ugh, still doing yoga, are we?" and leaving.

Mia was still banging on about becoming famous, not sure I've actually mentioned how ambitious some of her ambitions are, she's already telling friends she'll pay off their mortgage in a couple of years! And now Caris was around more, and nicer, she decided to give Mia a helping hand. She emailed a local radio station and a local magazine, asking if they'd like to do a piece about DID. Neither Caris nor Mia could believe that Amber was letting them do this, it gave Mia a welcome distraction from her misery though, maybe that was why.

And Jacob was back. He is I think the fastest 'processed' alter we've briefly got to know. So far, only he and Kai have been the opposite gender to the body and most of the system. It's very common though, and obviously can cause problems for alters who feel like they are in the wrong body.

Disconnection from the way the body physically looks is common, but this can be a whole other level of discomfort for some. Zac Efron is an introject who lives inside and we've met. Realised it was him when he sat watching himself over and over again singing The Other Side on The Greatest Showman. When he realised the situation, we had a chat, he understood, decided to take the body to bed - went and brushed the teeth, checked out the boobs, and went to sleep.

Anyway, Jacob.

> "Hello this is Jacob. I've aged to about 14 in the last few days, I started coming out a bit more maybe last weekend and then yesterday asked if I could make a Lego truck, i was about 8 then. I made the smaller one yesterday and the girls let me put on a documentary about castles which was ok and then last night I asked if I could make a bigger truck and then now I aged a bit more this morning, I remembered that Kai did and then he just went and lived inside with Cherry so I think maybe if I age I can just do that bc I don't really understand the point of any of this. Hope I can leave, Amber says I've been processing this morning while making my truck which is weird bc it's not like we know what we are processing or anything. Anyway either I shared this or Mia or Lolly or someone did so I decided to. Hopefully won't be around for much longer haha see ya! - Jake (oh wait I've aged and fused with Jake. Ok that makes sense. Cool. Lol. Someone is like yeah u know that makes no sense to anyone but us right)."

He literally aged, found his older self, fused with them, and became Jake - while writing that status. Seriously, if you have (or suspect you have) DID (or anything), find some way to spew it out. It needs to come out, and most of the time it won't make any sense. Make an anonymous private Instagram and just let it go. Journal. Draw. Scribble. We didn't even realise how much this was helping us, until I've come to put it all together and realise just how much we have written and processed this last year, thanks Mia.

So, Jacob is now Jake. He's aged, think he was in his twenties, he wasn't here (in his current form), for much longer.

> "Jacob's gone lol. He made his truck, kept thinking about how when he'd made his truck he'd be able to leave and not deal with this anymore. Then he went out for a dog walk, he was listening to Linkin Park lol (that was Kai's music of choice too!) After maybe 45 minutes or so he started thinking about Isabel, corrected himself to Caris, and she came out. They were both just there, almost like some long lost romantic nonsense and we're all like what on earth is going on here?!

> Then they realised they were the same person!! He must've been a split from Is at some point?! Anyway they fused and now he's with Caris! Thankfully that was a quick event and not a days-long fusion of anxious weirdness! So anyway, one more down, dog knows how many to go! - Mia!"

Yeah. I'm trying to remember how this felt for them. Oh, speaking of things I'm trying to remember, you remember how Stef had that big emotional event that ended her tyranny? I remembered what that was, and it was an old attachment trauma from when we were young. It took effort for me to find that information so I'm going to respect her privacy and leave it there.

Anyway! Weird. It really did feel romantic, there was a connection, souls finding each other, that love people describe, gazing deep into each other's eyes, getting lost, simultaneously finding yourself and another (OMG stfu - she is literally doing this to piss me off! Get on with it, dickhead - Caris). Me? Never. It was big, then they just go "Ok, should we fuse?", "Sure", job done.

And the latest wave of littles were having a good time:

> "We restarted Mia's rabbits! She got loads more now so we gotta come up wiff stories! We been haffing good time at granmas we got sticker book and a grocery store for sylvanians and Mia showed us animal crossing and that good! Lolly Sophie jasmine and tiger mostly inside they teenage not sure what's happening. We r ageing it Astrid I five now. Bye from Astrid and peach and faith and Gemma"

This was interesting - we kept suggesting to the littles they might like to play Animal Crossing, they really weren't bothered, said they didn't know how to and it was boring. We played AC for more than a thousand hours in 2020 (mostly in the lockdowns). How they could 'not know how to play', was pretty extraordinary, and related to how memories work we think. They couldn't be bothered to remember, effort, knowing what you're looking for, remembering things is actually hard. Mia managed to get them on AC though, and as soon as she'd shown them a few bits they were filling in the gaps themselves and having fun.

Around now (early November), was when Lolly, Sophie, Jasmine, Tiger, Carabel, and Abigail disappeared, and would be gone for about a month or so. It was hard, communication was very limited and they were clearly deep in TP inside, but it was difficult not knowing what was happening with them.

Peach, Astrid, Faith and Gemma weren't hanging around though. And one day, they recognised they were trauma processing, so they went and made a video for Berlou's YouTube channel, about it. It's extraordinary, the bravery, but also seeing them process trauma and working out what they need to do to let it go. In an eleven minute video they go from being in obvious physical discomfort to, well, not great, but much better. They sit and chat about their experience and what they know about TP. They sway, even unwind a bit. It's quite lovely.

The BIG fusion

The madness

By Mia

In the middle
She sat
Watching
The madness
Unfold
Until
It
Engulfed
Her
And she
Became

The best thing I can do here is let Caris tell you what happened, I'll try not to interrupt too much.

"Hi it's Caris,

We need to BLAH the last 24 hours and no one else is so I'm doing it here. It's epic obv.

So a few days ago Berlou mentioned she wanted to fuse with Amber again. She's been saying it since the beginning but always wanted to do her own thing first. So then it's 4am and she makes the decision a few nights ago. They pop off inside to see what happens.

A lot of confusion lol. They're both like are we fused not fused blended wtf is going on. Then yesterday happened with the littles holding the front most of the day playing, making YouTube videos apparently?! Wow. Oh ok so they processed a lot of what was going on with Berlou and Amber in the afternoon. This is getting stream of consciousnessy I apologise, I'm remembering as I type."

No worries, I do it too.

"So that's happened and in the evening they're watching some tv and do some twists working into the spine and chest. Then whoever was in the front got kicked out like pulled back. The body started unwinding itself (usually someone is in it when it's doing this! So we're still present just letting it do what it wants. This was the body literally seeming to take control of itself. Oh and unwinding is part of myofascial release and releases physically stored trauma). It wasn't big or drastic, just arm movements and movements around the torso, head and neck. Mia, Amber and whoever else was there couldn't get any control to even open the eyes or speak for a couple of minutes. Someone got into the face somehow and opened the eyes and felt it was related to Berlou and the first trauma. Then Berlou was there and she was then in the body going through parts of the first trauma again. And after not long she's done and she's sat there in the body obviously in shock. She'd aged again to about 34. Everything felt really strange and the body felt different to how she had ever experienced it, she realised she had never fully been in the body even when fronting alone. One guess about this is that the unwind was necessary before she could, it would be too painful for her while the body was still holding the trauma. (There have been three, I think, big unwinds related to it since Amber learnt about it while unwinding on a table in Chicago with 100 people two and a bit years ago).

So they go to bed. Wake at 4.30 maybe, awake for a couple of hours just not-remembering-what-I-was-just-thinking-about. Berlou chatted to Ben and realised she was talking about Amber as if she was Amber....

They examine themselves and realised they are fused and confused (you could do something with that, Mia, lol)."

I'm pretty sure there is a fused and confused poem somewhere, can't think which it is. Found it.

After

By unknown

Confusion
After
Fusion
Discomfort
But we know
We have each other

You want me to comment on the whole body taking control of itself and that we're making this nonsense up and you want to believe none of this can be true, because that means that there's a lot we don't know or understand and it's all so scary and surely modern medicine knows everything about everything already, and what on earth is this fascia and unwinding nonsense. Ok, I'm making this up. Let's carry on. YAY Berwoo is coming! I'm excited, and so is she, Caris?

"They get up to make tea and hear a little voice "I'm here"... so Amberlou (I'm joking I'm joking she's just gonna be Amber) and Mia are like 'oh god, here we go again'. "I'm here" "Come closer, you're too far away" "I'm here!" "I'm here" and bang - new little in the front ALL GRINS. "Sorry I'm late", Mia and Amber are like "What on earth who are you?!'' It's only Berlou!! Non-traumatised four year old! So she's somehow wrangled simultaneously living the grownup life with Amber and poofed herself back to little where she can actually enjoy it this time instead of constantly trauma processing!!!

Omg this brain. So we've been to yoga, very needed, and not much else. Amberlou are confused and going to take a few days to settle. They've a client tomorrow afternoon here they're hoping to be up to seeing. New Berlou has decided she might change her name to Baloo or Berwoo (Mia doesn't pronounce Ls so Berlou is Berwoo often).

Anyway Jason's squeaking. I'll take this chaos out for some nature. Thanks if you made it to the end and any of it made any sense, well done - Caris and Mia!"

She didn't see the client, I don't think. I have a feeling the universe helped us out and it was cancelled or rearranged by them, fortunately.

Making it up

By Mia

U want me to say
I'm making this up
I wish
I could
Say I am

Throughout this whole thing, somehow, they'd never had a bug or any other kind of 'poorly' to contend with (other than the constant trauma processing), but now they had a cold, and Mia was the one suffering, and reflecting on the impact hormones have upon the system.

"We r poorly! It's no good! Oh but I'm little again so it's not awful! Oh no I'm wrong it is awful! I think it's to do with Berlou (I always said she was trouble!!), some kind of that thing where when u stop u get ill? And the body goes yep nope no more But Ambers stupid brother did have a cold he possibly probably shared with us. So anyway we're gonna be lying around sneezing with lots of snot and period pain... oh re that, recently we've noticed events do happen during the beautiful phase of being premenstrual... it's like do hormones just tip us over the edge and make things happen or are we really cyclical and it's all related? We've always suffered with PMT so assume whatever is going on related to that always has and that's why we are especially crazy during those times. K bye pls send hankies hugs love sympathy healing goodness stickers and unicorns and I will be eternally grateful! From Mia!"

Blood, pain and misery

By Mia

Oh
Hello
You monthly
Hell

And, they heard back from the magazine Caris emailed!

"We got some exciting news but also basically dead from snot and coughing and sneezing, and Amber's been basically gone all day for the first time in AGES which is pretty poo. (Someone just added that comma above, don't correct my language thank u). So anyway Caris also emailed Now Then magazine which is a Sheffield magazine and a journalist who writes about women's stuff and health and mental health wants to do a bit about DID. So that's kinda fun. While Caris and I were emailing her we were waiting for Amber to come and be like nope nope nope but she actually just said something to the effect of "do what the fuck you want, I don't care anymore" so that's nice! She's ok I think honest lol but who knows bc you'd think I'd know but I actually don't know anything. Luff Mia"

But, it seemed that Berlou requesting to be fused with Amber, set off a chain of events that affected the whole system. Berlou was ageing and changing, others were changing against their will too. And when the actual fusion began, it was another few days of limited people being outside, feeling physically and mentally terrible, and not knowing what was happening or how long it would last. And Mia was stuck in the front, and little, again...

Shopping

By Miya

Would you like me to go and do the shopping for you?
I didn't know I had to shop!
I can't shop!
Yeah
You're poorly I can go shop
IT'S NOT BECAUSE I'M POORLY
IT'S BECAUSE I'M SEVEN

She had also just discovered how much more she enjoyed processing using language when she made it prettier, this was one of her first poems.

Fusion

By Mia

Constant flux
Never stable
Tears of sadness
Sit on my face
Lonely
And confused
I wish
I wish I was more
I wish I was less
I wish I was whole
Instability in my self

Shifting people
Finding their ways
Together
In the dark
We hold hands and hope
Wait for the relief
That comes after
Knowing beneath
They're cutting and sticking
Putting us back together
While I wait
Heavy chest
Eyes they cry
Breathing is hard
I want it to be over
They know not when
They send messages of hope
Of dreams
Of a better time
My selves I know will come back
I don't have to be here much longer
Alone
My family will come back stronger
Hopefully with the next sunrise
Bringing brightness and hope
Love and light
Holding me tight

This poem, we don't know if her writing it was affecting inside, but Amber and the others came back soon after she wrote it. And Berwoo was already hilarious.

Back

By Mia

She was back
But
She didn't know
Who she was
It took a minute
Uncomfortable
In her skin
She asked
For help
I said
I don't know
Who you are
Berwoo said
Ur name is
Geraldine
What
Yes
Geraldine
Hahaha only joking ur Amber
Oh
Wow
Then
She complained
That I hadn't washed clothes
Hadn't showered
She
Shouldn't leave me then
Should she

Yup, Amber was confused, she was 'becoming', alright.

"Seems like Amberlou are more present. It's not a strong presence though and Mia was just thinking about doing a post herself "Well, Amber's back but tbh it's pretty underwhelming" Amber: "fuck you". There seems to be a lot of "fuck yous" happening atm. - Caris and Berwoo and Mia"

And Mia had other complaints too.

"Oh because of that damn Berlou and all her messing around ageing fusing healing I'm definitely NOT 7 year old atm. It's kinda fun because I can swear but being little is definitely 100% better than being bigger. And I'm super envious that Berwoo opened with a joke, that is how to make your entrance to the physical world - Mia obv"

Remember

By Berlou and Miya

Do you remember
Dancing to this song
In the head
At yoga?

Fuck
You

And more complaints.

"One of the absolute worst things is just not understanding why we feel like we do. We lay around all morning in bed and watched some series of extraordinary events, which is working quite well as a distraction. I asked for peas and mint from the supermarket to make some pea soup. Managed to get out of bed, Berwoo and whoever played some animal crossing and then I went to make my pea soup. I've no idea what happened inside but in the time I'd taken the compost out, done some dishes and made my soup I was getting more and more uncomfortable. Came to slice some bread and just had to come upstairs to cry. So my soup's downstairs and I'm hungry but so very very sad and just want to cry. I know it's Berlou and Amber but it's so hard being with it. I want my soup. I feel like Amber is disappointed in me and embarrassed but I know she isn't and I don't know what that feeling is about. I think that's more I think she would be embarrassed about me and is my own projection, combined with this sadness that's spewing out from inside us. So I'm processing their stuff out here for them and my own lol. We got some vicks which made the littles happy. Mia."

And more complaints, but someone was listening, even if they couldn't help.

"U no all that stuff about doing shadow work and finding yourself and the collective consciousness, where does leaving your life and letting someone else run the show for a while fit in to all this? Hi it's Caris (that was Mia) She's ok. Well she's not ok but whatever we're doing we need to do, the Amber-Berlou fuse was always going to be a massive event and it's just a fucker that Mia's stuck out here with Berwoo and we're poorly. I wish I could stay and make it easier for her but I can feel myself being pulled back again. Mia - you're a hero, just keep going, everyone will be back soon I promise! At times these amnesiac blocks are so frustrating! You'd think after a year of figuring the logistics of this out we'd have sussed a workaround. But nope. We're quite literally still in the dark - Caris. She gone. That nice I guess. Just keep swimming. - Mia."

Eventually...

"She's back. I happier."

But, there were more surprises...

"Good morning!

We r exhausted obv. And there's more changes than we thought/ expected here. A while after Amber had been back last night we realised Caris is with her too… so Amber is now: Amber, Pen, Isabel, Cara, Jake, Berlou and Alex. As the assumed goal for therapy is often unification I guess this is a good thing! We're still a we obv, Stef, me and Maya, Berwoo, and the littles and teens are still separate (plus whoever else lol).

Definitely going to take some time to work out if this will work. Berlou and Amber aren't sure about being Isabel and Isabel isn't sure about being present all the time. But they're all really old parts - Berlou's been here since we were 2, Isabel at least 3, Pen we think 2, Cara at least 5, Jake was a split from Is, Alex a split from Amber when we were 11.

Amber dragged us for a longish dog walk and now we're playing/ hopefully sleeping some more. Someone said a poem I wrote last night and put on our Instagram was good so obv this morning I've made another insta for our writing/poetry. Amber says we don't need more projects, but what does she no lol. I called it did.we.write, and then I wrote this for my first post!

How do u no
If ur good enough
To write poetry
It no matter
U write for u
Taking the words
Out of the brain
The feelings
They change as the words leave
As the light hits the words
They shine
They resonate
The brain can see the words
It makes more sense
So I write for me

I make the words
I feel them go from thought
To finger
Tap tap
Letter letter
Feeling feeling
Transformed

I'll pop my one from last night in the comments, it was about how I was feeling when Amber was gone again.

Mia obv and BERWOOOOOOO! Oh yeah she's here too!!"

A new obsession, one I could help with: the descent into writing mania began.

Writing, writing, writing

Autonomy

By Miya

She achieved
Extraordinary
Healing
And said
"I want to live the life
I want to host"
To give up
Her autonomy
Be present
Mostly

So
They fused
But
Others joined too
They weren't
Strong enough
Alone

She is now
Many people
Fused

Stuck together
Thinking
As one

She feels like herself
But thinks
Like others
Sometimes

After the fusion, things were strange for everyone. The hardest part to accept was Caris unexpectedly joining Berlou and Amber. When Amber (plus plus) realised Caris was with them. The only person they knew would understand (as much as anyone else could), was the Extra System. The following dialogues came from the brand new alter, Camberlouis (see what I did there? Cara, Amber, Berlou, Isabel - I don't care what anyone says, Mia and I are geniuses).

Reconciliation

By Amber and Mia

How
Will I ever
Reconcile
Being
Isabel
Stfu bitch
U luff me

Caris, like Mia, thinks she's a lot funnier than she actually is.

Being Isabel

By Amber and Miya

I dunno
It's weird
I'm so many people
Like
Isabel
Used to
Vibrate with anger
Anticipation of a threat
She's different now
Calmer
But
It's still weird being her

Aw, we've finally mentioned The Extra System. I have a Mia poem here, about our friendship with them. We can message each other anytime, about anything, doesn't matter how bizarre it is. They're priceless.

Extra

By Mia

The Extras
It's not the best name
They're our friend
They might be
Any number of people though
Well, about 30 or so
So we just call them The Extras
They were
One of the first system friends
We made
They're a bit younger than us
Which Amber sometimes finds awkward
We made friends

Because they have a Mia
When Mia's around we have Mia parties
WHERE WE CAPS UNTIL SOMEONE TELLS US NOT TO
WE USE too many emojis
It's good fun when Mia's here
Sat
She's like our Stef and Is
Inappropriate
Protective
She'd kick your ass
We know
Who they are
And they know
Who we are
From just a few messages
It's nice
To have that validation
We both
Go through our miserable lives
We laugh
Together
About
SH
And suicide
What?
You laugh?
Sometimes you have to
I'm glad we have someone
We can laugh
At the sheer desperation
Of a
Situation
With

We luff u

She wrote about other friends, too.

Friends

by Miya

We're watching
It
Again
It's comforting
The brain
Knows
What's going
To happen
We don't
Have to pay attention
Can
Play
Write
Chat
It
Makes us smile
We
Like them
I think
We just don't
Have any space
For new information

Mia and Berwoo collaborated.

T

By Mia and Berwoo

T
Tra la la
Can be
Anything
U can ask
A TH
What T
Is to her
I can ask
A TH
What it is to her?

Tra la la
It in ur skin
In ur bones
But when
U separate
The body
And the mind
And the
T

It becomes
Compartmentalised
Separate
U
Can
Leave
It
Somewhere else

It confusing
It always there
But magic
(Dissociation)
Means it blurry
Like a jigsaw
The pieces
Separate
They don't fit

A jigsaw
That spent
Years
Being thrown around
Made and broken
Time and time
Again

So the pieces
Don't fit
U try
To fix it
But
All the edges
Are frayed

U try
To fix the
Pieces
It's hard
They don't stay still
They

All shake
When u get close

But
U keep trying
To smooth the edges
Love them
Take the T
And transform it
Into
Something else

The pieces
Become clearer
And as they
Soften
And smooth
They find
They can fit together

It's hard tho
And scary
And it hurts
The pieces
Have been
So battered
So bruised
They itch
They don't no each other
They irritate

It takes
Time

Patience
Love
They try
To share
To smooth together
With time
The pieces
Soften

Love
They need
Understanding
The knowledge
They can take
All the time
In the world

A lesson
In
Patience

But
They learn
To be together
To function
As one

With time
The pieces
Smooth
The pain
Subsides
The anxiety

Is released
They learn
To live together
To love each other

And, Jason got his own poem, of course, no one could have got through this year without him.

Jason

By Miya

Somehow
He always knows
Before the tears even fill the eyes
He's looking
Watching
Asking
What's wrong
Do u need me
Here
Touch me
It will help
And I like it
It sounds
Dramatic
To say
Without our dogs
We might be dead
But
So
Many
Times
She's kept going

For them
Their love
Incomparable
I love my Jason
He's my best friend
Always hopeful
Bullies us in the kitchen
For biscuits
Or frozen peas
Waits until he thinks we're asleep
To sneak on the bed
Makes us walk
Every
Day
We speak a language
We can't hear
It
Is
Love

There

By Mia

U cud giff up
No one
Wud
Blame u

But
What if
It
Gets better

It wont
Be easy
But
One day

One hour
One minute
One second
At a time

U
Will
Get
There

We
Will
Get
There

Assessment

I don't think I'll need to be here for much of this chapter, though I might clarify the odd thing. This was now the second waiting list they'd been on, and they were still waiting to hear how long it was. The first had been for a General Mental Health Assessment (or something like), which the lovely MH nurse we see advised us, was not the one we wanted to be on. That was just a gateway assessment before you get to speak to someone with qualifications.

Amber rang the Single Point of Access (SPA - super clear name, this is the organisation within the NHS that deals with all mental health stuff in Sheffield) many, many times. Explaining that she has DID, they have correspondence from her doctor, a MH nurse she sees, drug counsellor, and therapist supporting this and she didn't want to go through the stress of an extra and unnecessary assessment. Eventually someone rang her back and confirmed she had switched waiting lists. They had no idea how long this list was though. This was back in July, they'd been on the first list since February, so they were getting used to the waiting game.

They got a big surprise mid-November though.

Assessment tomorrow

By Mia

I cannot play
We r in shock
Soon

We learn
We be told
We have someone else
Outside
Tell us
What we are
We want to know
Labels
They get
A bad rep
But they can help
As long
As they don't
Use them against u
U can no who u r
Better
When someone says
Yes
Ur experience fits
U r right
Even tho we no
We no when it started
We no how it started
We no why it started
But we don't no
Why the brain
Chose to do this
But we aren't alone
Our experience
Is unique
But comparable
We see others
And say

They like us
We like them
It helps
To no
Altho we r alone
We r not alone
And maybe tomorrow
We
Will be able to say
We have DID
Not we think we
Have DID
Hopefully

There had been a cancellation, were they free, tomorrow, to speak to a psychiatrist at 11.15am on the phone? Absofuckinglutely. Maya took the phone call, confusing the woman on the other end of the line saying she wasn't Amber, of course.

And, sleep was still something other people did.

Anticipation

By Mia

It's something
And nothing
It will
Not
Change
Anything
And yet
It might change everything
Waiting

The scenarios
Float through
The headspace
Sleep
What is sleep
It will make no difference
Except
For
Us
It might
Bring clarity
Validity
Confirmation
It comes
At
The
Perfect
Time
For us
To fly

They didn't sleep much. Awoke at four am. And Amber was now many, and had to process with words herself. Mia let her do it on their account, now she was one of them too.

"Ok I need to do the word blah thing, it's Amber (/Caris/Berlou).

As Mia's advised everyone here, I'm now a few different people. It's all a bit strange. We're fused, we think, at least we're stuck together and mostly think seamlessly. I'm still mostly feeling like Amber. But at times I think/say things more Berlou or Caris would think/say.

We often think one of the most important qualities necessary for this to have been revealed is openness... and without Amber's (yes I can speak about myself in third person IT'S WEIRD) almost submission to the process, it would have been impossible, or at least taken much longer.

Fascinatingly (to us lol) I have somehow spent years laying the groundwork for this reveal. The tools I've gathered; hypnotherapy, myofascial release, yoga, trauma processing, dogs, nature... all were literally required for us to do this. And I noticed last night, it happened after I opened myself to spirituality (I'm not about to say they're ghosts and I'm a medium lol, don't worry), and, energy. Seriously, it was after I got my second reiki attunement (a little ceremony that "connects" you to energy) that it started going wild. Seven months after that I was in America, finding Berlou. Self at least has an energetic component, of that we're convinced.

And wow this assessment today. Also wow the phone call didn't trigger me out, that says two things: 1. I was deep again but this time it was ok because Mia had found Maya and had someone else with her, and 2. Wow, there is no way that Maya could take two important phone calls a few months ago so we're all in awe at how she managed yesterday morning. Mia found her by accident when she wanted to reply to a Facebook post but wanted someone older to do it for her, usually it's Caris she'd call but that's not an option now, so she was like "I just need an older me?". And a few seconds later Maya was writing. She's been very present since, so we're hoping she will be around more now.

And yeah. Assessment. We will see how that goes. Thinking we'll just let Berwoo (MORE ridiculous than Mia) tell the story. Ok I'm done.

Amber (version God only knows - we assume this splitting and fusing has been going on forever, we just obviously had no idea before we knew. And explains a lot)."

Isabel was finding it difficult not having her independence. She felt like whenever she followed and explored her own thoughts Amber would 'scoop her back', (the best way she could describe it). This was Amber's experience with Caris a couple of days after the fusion.

Separate

By Amber and Miya

She tried to
Separate
She was
Thinking by herself
Playing with
Independence

Bang
The head
Intense pressure
Pushed
And pulled
Almost
Unbearable

I said
Stop
She did
She
Came back to us
Leaving
Heavy sensations
Awareness

It wouldn't
Be
Surprising
If she just
Poofs

Back
Out

We'll see

It was already becoming obvious that at least the Caris-Amber aspect of the fusion was unlikely to last. We've seen other systems speak of switching or presence headaches, and feel this experience of Caris pushing back, the pressure in the head was painful, it might be comparable, or one of the reasons for headaches. Fighting it would definitely be bad. That morning, they wrote, went to yoga, got home, showered, and were ready by the phone with a few minutes to spare.

Waiting

By Mia

We sit here
We wait
Why
Does
It
Take
So
Long
The anxiety
Is strong
People
Are present
Physically
Shaking
Anticipation
Expectation
Hope

He does not
Call

I don't know if you know anxiety, but if something important is happening at 11.15, and it's 11.30, and you have a lot of anxious people, all waiting, all together, all desperate. It gets rough. She rang them, spiralled, and half an hour after he was going to ring, he rang.

Dinosaur

By Mia

Mpd
He says
That's not even
A thing
It's been DID
For
Decades

Dinosaur
Of course we got
A dinosaur
He quotes knowledge
From the
80s
He tells us
Where to find
Leaflets
Cause that's
What we
Need
A leaflet
On anxiety

I swear to dog
I no
More than he does
He says
He's treated
Thousands of
Dissociation patients
But
Does not know
How to
Talk to one

I sit
On hold
Waiting
To find out
What
He
Said
Because
We can't remember

D
I
S
S
O
C
I
A
T
I

O

N

Ud think

He could grasp

The concept

They don't no

We

Wait

Mia told you what happened. It was bad. Unstructured, he was unpleasant, he had no grasp of what dissociation was, yet is probably an expert in his field. It was horrific. Mia knew what to do to process though.

Chocolate

By Mia

Chocolate

Haha

Joking

This isn't

About chocolate

It's about

Chocolate

Beauty and the beast

Animal crossing

Jason

The body

It tingles

Vibrates

Buzzes

Sensations

Popping
Fire
Ice
Contractions
Tremors

We see
It is
The release
Of

T
R
A
U
M
A

It's better out
Now
Than in
For another
30 years
So I sit here
I play my game
I watch my Disney
I eat my chocolate
I love my Jason
And I feel
While
My body
Let's go
Of this morning

And Amber let it tap tap out of the fingers, too.

"Obviously the assessment was an absolute shit show, and not the easy diagnosis we were way too optimistically hoping for. According to the wonderful old consultant psychiatrist (if this turns into a Mia poem, I'm sorry):

DID is rare.
DID cannot be diagnosed in the UK as it doesn't exist in the whatever tf manual that isn't the DSM that is used in the UK. (How are people getting a diagnosis then?)
DID is more common in developing countries (no shit it's caused by trauma, why are we talking about this?)
DID is not so common in developed countries. (Yawn)
DID is rare. (OK.)
DID affects more women than men. (Yawn)
In the UK it is still MPD (wtaf, I have no idea at this point)
DID does not affect 1-3% of the population, but 0.1-1%.
BTW, DID is rare.
I have a number of dissociative disorders.
I might have a diagnosis (I was dissociating hard and Mia was trying to keep things going but failing).
He's writing to my GP.
He cannot send the report to me.

Fortunately, during the subsequent meltdown my phone reminded me we had an appointment with the mental health nurse, THANK DOGS. So he's going to keep an eye out for the report, if it's a diagnosis we can see where we go from here, if it's something else he's going to complain and ask for a second opinion.

He's going to email me when the report comes through, and gave me his email address to email him whenever... I was like be careful, Mia will take that at face value and she will email you, he's like yeah that's fine just get her to sign it.

Got another appt on the 22nd Dec with the MH nurse, as we're leaving Mia's says "Alwight bye then! Oh nex appointment is near my birthday it's Christmas Eve, you'd better get me a present, I like Sylvanian Families and Lego"... - Amberlouis. I can make name jokes too."

Nah, Caris makes name jokes, not Amber, oh, Caris is Amber, I'm confused. And, Stef decided to 'join the party' (Amber was not happy about the terminology.)

My two cents

By Stef

Hi it's Stef
I've not been here
For a while
It's funny
I find
This arrangement
Of thoughts
Prepared
We can think
If we choose to
Like Mia's poems
So
Having never written more than a status update
I find myself
Feeling like I can
Write poetry?

The experience
Of being multiple
Means
I've been here

For 5 minutes
But can say
"What a day"
Atm
I don't even really know
What's happened
But I feel it
And as I ask
It is filled in
The sadness
And immediately battered
Hopes
When his first words
Were invalidating
Leading questions
In spite
Of seeming
Nice
Ish
The repeated return to
Insinuating
It was researched
And
Subsequently
Manifested
In spite
Of
Berlou
And the T

But
Mia's been processing hard
She's the warrior

They will recover
Quickly
She is on a mission
She won't slow
We have no choice

I know in myself
I'm not here much
And here
There have been
Fusions
I find myself
Wondering
"Should I join the party?"
In spite
Of just saying
I'm glad I have it cushy
Wherever I've been
It has to have been
Better than here
But
Am I maybe
Missing out

They tried to find out what happened during that phone call, but no one would tell them. Amber somehow saw the positive though, that it was giving Mia the material she wanted! As you can imagine, sharing a brain with Mia can be... a lot? At times.

"Mia is literally spewing poetry atm.

I'm trying to settle after a big fusion last week and we unexpectedly got an assessment, which went as you'd expect and not as we hoped. We *might* have a diagnosis of something, possibly multiple personality disorder, which isn't even a thing anymore. So we're waiting to find out what the hell is happening with that.

Anyway, Mia is writing god knows how many poems a day. She sorted an Instagram and another fb page (both DID we write) and is putting them there."

And Amber wasn't doing that great either...

Real

By Mia

She's decided she isn't real
She is being written in a book
By a seven year old narrator
I *think* she's joking
But send help

So, all sorts of weird stuff happening inside, waiting to hear about this diagnosis outside, it wasn't the best time (not that it ever is the best time).

"We a mess. We cleaned. Amber finding it hard. Biggest change for her yet and we no slept well for like 20 years and omg the head hurts so bad. I shud be asleep (yeah that was actually gonna happen lol) but I had words I needed to get out. Amber tried writing before but it's hard - she can't easily talk about the fusion bc she is now all the people involved. "And so I fused with me and then me and me etc"

Anyway I wrote a poem but cba to make it look pretty for my Instagram atm but wanted to share so here it is. Not sure of it's name yet - Mia."

She named it 'Sacrifice', it's good, needed to be closer to the beginning of the book, but here it is again, unedited (not sure how much it was edited, other than paragraphs).

I often worry
About
The sacrifices Amber made
For us to be us
Me to be me
For this to have
Come this far
The openness
The acceptance
The willing to be weird
It's hard
She says
She hasn't done anything
All she did
Was let it happen
She
She
I know
I'm strange
I'm not like u
I don't have a birth certificate
I don't have my own experiences
Before Christmas Eve
Last year
I have memories of a life not mine
I've had to suffer
It's easier to
Cope with pain
Smol
So I speak strange
And I play
I post too much

I try to
Be strong
And we've all suffered
Amber has lost friends
And made friends
And found a family inside
Separated
By strong imaginary veils
We're here now tho
She lets us be
And yes she's been lucky
Circumstance
Allows
Us time
To heal
Messily
She
Allows
Us
To heal messily
And be seen
Do u no what it means to be seen?
U might no what it means to be not seen
It's hard
It creates doubt
Uncertainty
Pain
I wonder how many
Others
Wish to be seen
That's one reason I shout
It's not just see me
But see others

Oh, I see
It took a minute
That's why
She lets me be
She also knows
Suppression
Goes
Badly
Whatever the reasons
I'm grateful
To be
And
To be seen

And Mia was still visibly processing as she was writing.

Extreme

By Mia

We r
Extreme
But u no
It's for
Good
Reasons

Isabel
Warrior
U laff
But
When uv
Only experienced
Pain

Fear
Frustration
All u c
Are

T
H
R
E
A
T
S

Everywhere

U
Don't no
That
What u c
Is
Filtered
The light
Is gone

U
Must
Fight

Maya
Can
Be
No
One

Because
She had to be

Berlou
Cried

I
Am
Extreme
U
C
Me
U
Think
Why
How
Wtaf
But
Haff u helped heal

Berlou
Alex
Maya
Jas
Lola
Soph
Pen

By
Becoming one with them
Showing them

Life

Can

Be

Good

Helped to heal

Amber

The alter

And

Amber

The whole

We

R

All

Extreme

Amber

Had

To balance

A lot

So yes it was hard

And we r sorry

We are currently, at the time of writing, just moving poems around. Amber's here; she's in shock at what we've created. Anyway, this would ordinarily go in the notes for future confusion, but she really is, ok, wait, this is probably a massive writing faux pas (the whole book is, I know), but she says: "Looking at it. 189 pages. In both, a year and a month. Maya's poem 'Chandelier' keeps echoing. I think you are right, Jessica. You will make this beautiful. And I think it has the potential to help a lot of people. I love all three of you. Amber" Ha, three. You don't know about the twist that we don't even know about here where these poems are in time, the third writer.

Mia Maya

By Mia/Miya

Maya and I
We split 2 days
After we came out
I
Forced
Her
Out

She was uncomfortable
Had older thoughts
Worries
Anxieties
Likes
Interests
I
Just wanted
To be
Little

So
We split
She became older
Anxious
I Became younger
Me

Now I see
She's been
Around more
At times

I've felt older
And gone
Bleugh
But maybe
We're blendy

Maybe
We've
Healed
Enough

If Isabel can become Amber
Then I guess
I can be Maya too
We
Will
See

Not much time later...

Growing up

By Mia

F*ck
Me and Maya
Might fuse
Might have fused
The
Thoughts
Have been floating
Around for a while
And now
I think

She's just being quiet
I feel
Different
Oh
Ffs
Before
We fused
And split
Two days later
Upon Ambers instruction
I wonder if enough has changed
I'm not sure I'm ready to be a grown up
I've managed to mostly avoid it for almost a year
So why now

This is the edited version, in the middle of it there was this beautiful piece of prose...

I wanted to make a TikTok with Maya last time we split
Taylor Swift
We are never ever getting back together
Duet
Lol
Dammit
This is half poem half status update
I'm not subjecting insta to it
Stef is Amber too now!
There's no one left
Oh
Cherry says hi lol
Ok I can definitely age slide so it's ok

Oh yeah, I forgot Stef was around again. After her saying she was wondering about joining the big old front fusion, in a poem, inevitably the next day they realised that she had joined the party. (Yep, still getting a bad vibe from Amber about that). I think this is Amber, she seems to have started using the alter Facebook account and not signing off - guess it's difficult when you're a few different people, to decide who you are.

> "I remembered Mia asked a few weeks ago to be fused with Jessica, the writer who appeared when Mia asked for one to journal for her (there are definite 'families' of alters who we assume can easily fuse and split, and have been doing so forever). Jessica at the time said no, but I just realised no one has noticed her presence for a while, got someone outside to ask if Miya (Mia and Maya fused again yesterday, hopefully more successfully than last time) was Jessica, and she laughed a lot as she said yes. So that kinda explains the poetry."

Yup, they found me. Honestly I said no to Mia! She asked me if I'd do it, so she could write. I said no, absolutely no way would I want to be Mia (it is the general consensus. Oi! - Disgruntled Mia!)

As you've probably gathered, we don't know how any of it works, but we assume over there, in the other side, we know more than we do here. Anyway someone decided it was happening and at some point Mia and I fused and she started writing day and night... And Mia, suddenly, had a book of poetry on her hands. But, being the wild creative she is, it was a mess.

How long

By Stef

For how long
Will we
Have to
Do this

The Troll and the book

The book

By Miya Squirrel

Do u want to write this book?
She says
I say yes
She says
Why haven't you sorted out your poems?
Ummmmmmmm
U cud?
No
Ummm I do it tomorrow?
Ooh!
Berwoo!
Will u sort my poems pls?
Into finished
And unfinished
Yes!
With Peach!
And Astrid!
She can't believe
I
Delegated
smug

She enlisted the help of the littles, who willingly sorted her poems into finished and unfinished, book and social media. Miya was Instagramming hard, constantly writing poems, posting at least a couple of times a day, and, of course, she got trolled. She cried, told Facebook she didn't think she had the strength. She was given so much love and encouragement that she was back at it in no time. Amber took to Facebook to thank everyone, and, after doubting and not being fully supportive of a lot of what Miya had been doing all the time...

> "And I'm gonna stop questioning what she's doing, maybe easier said than done lol. The constant narration is a bit old and hearing "there's a poem there!" 20 times a day ok ok now I'm supportive! Let's find those poems and make a book and live on Instagram."

And Miya said:

> "I fink she's trying to be helpful but she's just laughing at me! It's no good Amber, Stef and Isabel being togeffer they're all confused about what they think about things. Fanks effryone I really appreciate it. You are all wonderful humans."

And the next day, guess who was back to (one of) her old selves...

> "Hi it's Caris lol
>
> I woke up. Or at least I realised I was me after lying awake for a while. A few things:
>
> 1. This doesn't mean the fusion was a failure. We were uncomfortable some of the time and fusions do change things even if they don't last - look at Miya and her countless being other people lol. (And now she just randomly asks if people want to fuse with her she asked Tiger yesterday)

2. Omg my fav thing is that she says "why all you "alters" wrote same way did you all learn bad poems from same teachers?" NO WE WENT TO DIFFERENT SCHOOLS
3. Also I think it's probably blatantly obvious to anyone who knows anything about writing or English that Miya is by no means a literary scholar and is having fun expressing herself (and healing us) with words
4. Amber's gonna be like yeah I knew you'd leave me
5. I wonder where Stef is
6. Why is no one talking to me in my head "we're asleep. Go to sleep"
7. I think I'm Stef too
8. I'd better not be Amber confused
9. I need someone outside to ask me who I am

Ok I'll try for sleep.

- someone I think Caris and Stef but not sure

Edit: I think we know now who got the first class degree and why Amber spent her final year of uni stoned! (Pen - Mia is a version of Pen, and Pen was a non-traumatised alter created early to be able to have fun and achieve I guess - looking at Miya's current ambitions it is clearly the same attitude as when we were doing our degree, learning massage, moving to fucking Belgium, etc).

Edit 2: found Amber, Stef is still with her. Miya's happy I'm myself again."

Ok, a few things, Amber called it, Isabel was never gonna last. Honestly Caris's first agenda was to read everything the troll wrote herself and laugh at her a lot, while fuming. Oh, I have a poem she wrote, Mia didn't want to use it but I'll find it.

Stupid bitch

By Caris

Still simmering slowly
Hackles high
She with
No understanding of grammar
Dared to troll Miya
She can
Fuck
Right
Off
One version
Of Miya
Was once told
She writes
To
PhD standard
Miya chooses
To write like this

The whole Miya asking Tiger to fuse thing was actually pretty sweet. She was feeling all vulnerable because of what the troll had said, and thought 'Stef's tough, I wonder if Tiger is tough too and then I won't care what people think'. And yeah we already knew Pen got Amber's degree and is the biggest stoner. Sadly for Miya, Caris has an amazing habit of turning up, just to laugh at someone.

"Just realised Miya's poems are like they are because that's basically the extent of her attention span. First draft of the book is done. She's planning a poetry novel but happy with what she's put together now. We can't work out if we're really biased or it's an interesting insight into being multiple. She got Cherry out because she's never here to get fresh eyes. Caris"

It wasn't just Caris who had something to say about Miya...

Miya: "Amber just described me as a computer program. Not sure how to feel about this!"

Amber: "She is though! I've been through this determined, ambitious, obsessive (possibly manic I'm not sure, I did wonder for a long time if my problem was bipolar) thing God knows how many times in my life. Miya's a version of Pen... no idea what number version but a version... She and Caris are about to go through the book again then I'm to submit to the agents Caris listed yesterday, Caris was going to but then was like uh I think this needs to come from you? I guess I have the body's name. I wrote the email this morning. I don't know if this is ridiculous or not, but we are all along for the Miya ride."

Miya: "I'm doing this! No one can stop me! Not the negative ninnies in my head or my concerned granma or the trolls!"

Amber: "Yeah, the Miya ride."

Diagnosis

Diagnosis

By Miya

Mixed dissociative (conversion) disorder
Because
That
Explains
The
Manic seven year old
Who won't stop writing
In my head
She said

"Amber spoke to docs. They gots report from psych but can't tell us what it says. She got pretty upset. The psych told us to talk to docs. I email our nice mh nurse now and we ring the people that did the assessment tomorrow see if they can tell us. She told me I had to have a break from my writing work so we made cookies. - Mia"

Yep, almost a week later, they rang the doctors and found they had the report there, finally. The receptionist needed to speak to a doctor and would call them back. Rang SPA, can they tell us what it says? Do we have a diagnosis? They can't tell us, we need to talk to our doctor. Speak to a doctor, she can't tell us, we need to talk to the person who wrote the report. Ok, the one who says we've been discharged back to our doctors care... Yeah, it wasn't going well. Fortunately, the mental nurse got back to Mia.

> "We've been diagnosed with mixed dissociative conversion disorder. I've googled and am still clueless.
>
> Edit: maybe worked it out. He's decided the trauma releasing unwinding we described are seizures. The rest of it makes no sense and is no way relatable to our experience. He's a fucking idiot and it's devastating this man is likely a professional in his field and has been fucking up people's lives for years. I don't like swearing but he's a fucktard. Mia."

Yeah, Mia's either older or Caris is with her. Don't think I've mentioned that Mia's said a few times, "you know when I'm older, because I start fucking". She's talking about using the word, but this is an instance of Mia enjoying using innuendo and pretending she's no idea what she just said.

It was deduced that the insightful psychiatrist decided that the trauma processing Amber described was seizures, maybe. The 'conversion' part means it's somatic in nature, which yeah it is but it's also DID (Caris is with me, I wanted to write 'dickhead'). We will find out more on the 22nd of December when we meet with the mental nurse again. (It's the 9th now, and this was three weeks ago at the time of writing, just FYI.)

Unicorn

By Miya

Trying to get
A diagnosis
So u can
Get help
Is like
Trying to
Find a

Golden unicorn

The body

by Miya

I don't know what to do
We close the eyes
It's chaos
Can't rest
We open the eyes
Exhaustion
Fatigue
We yearn for sleep
But it alludes us
Always
The body
Is crying
We finally fed it
It still says it's tired
The brain won't stop
I take it
For a bath

Blah, blah, everything is boring and awful, but someone was ready for some long overdue fun, and was joining Mia in her writing work...

"Miya so naughty! Amber told her no more writing today. She can make notes but no big writing. Then Miya says she wants to tell my story and Amber like oh fine whateffer! Miya told my story in her poems! I luff it she say I saving them now by being me and being happy! That makes me feel nice inside. I hope I help us lots and I did my own poems today even tho we so v tired I did do some nice things I ate lots cookies and wrote my poems and did a little bit of animal crossing. Tomorrow be better from Berwoo!"

Berwoo

by Miya

Berwoo
You might think
That's a strange name
Let me tell u
Her story
She is a version
Of Berlou
And she
Cried for 36 years
Inside the head

When we found her
After Amber accepted us
She cried and cried
Amber Louise
She said her name was
Or, Berlou, for short
She couldn't cope
Overwhelm
All the time
We all worked hard

With time
And love
And patience
She started to heal
She shared
What made her cry
We wept with her

I even
Became one with her
For a while

It took
A lot of painful work
But Berlou
Healed
She aged
All she wanted
Was to help others
Like her
Who might be crying
In someone else's head

So Amber
Gave us permission
To be open
To share our
Story
And experiences
So we could maybe
Help others
Who couldn't understand
What was happening to them

Berlou had expressed that she
Would want to become
One with Amber
Fuse
To not miss anymore
Of the life
Recently she decided

It was time
Amber agreed
They waited to see what happened next

The fusion took days
Others joined
Trauma sharing
Alters missing
Discomfort and anxiety
Outside
Wondering what was happening
Inside
Eventually
They came back

In just over a year
Of finding out
We are a we
Our first and only
Major trauma holder
Had healed
Aged
And fused
With our host
She's our hero

While this was all going on
Someone new appeared
"I'm here!"
She shouted
"Come closer"
We said
She eventually got to us

"Sorry I'm late!"
She exclaimed
"Wtaf who are you?" we said

I'm Berlou!
But no trauma!
I'm Berwoo!
Wow
We said
This brain
I'm glad she's here
We need her more than ever now
We saved her
Now she's saving us

Splitting

Undone

By Stef

Miya says poem it
The fusions are coming undone
And yet
They feel like they were meant to be
I came back
In the bath
Realised I was me
I don't know
Where Amber is
I'm not sure
What's going on
With Isabel
Her scars keep itching
But we have learned
What it's like to be Amber
Hopefully
We can be more help now

Yep, they were putting Amber through hell. It was all necessary though, all this fusing and splitting and sharing and trauma - it was all progress and healing. Every fusion had benefited someone, they were bringing understanding and closeness to the system. It was becoming evident that their immediate goal would not be unification. They just needed to be able to live together, hopefully in relative harmony.

Separate

By Mia

I think it's better
Separate
We can leave
Easier
There are less people
Thinking
In the consciousness

Belief

By Miya

She believes
We've been
Splitting
And
Fusing
Forever
Without
Knowing

Well, obv

Crisis

by Miya

But, seriously

What is the point

What
Is
The
Point

Existential crisis
She says
U'll get over it

It be ok

By Berwoo

It be ok
Miya
Amber
We keep going
We gots each uffer
Ur strong
Ok
Miya
Gots problems
We
Work it out
Let's go nap

A strange morning confirmed that Mia/Miya and Amber probably don't want to become one, either.

Blurry

By Miya

We wake
Blurry
Where
Do I end
And you
Begin
Can we have
Healed
With words
I
Don’t want to
Be you
And
You
Don’t want to
Be me

Miyamber

By Miya

Yuck
It was
Horrible
Together
A blurry mess
Too distinct
To both be

Unexpectedly connected
Unable to communicate

One
Or the
Other
She can be
Her
And her
And her
But
Cannot be
Me

Phew
I say
I don't want
To be you either

I don't think I need to explain anything, it was unpleasant for all. And Mia's always said she doesn't want to be Amber because she's 'too boring', and Amber says she doesn't want to be Mia, understandably. Cherry popped out at some point. Honestly, I have no idea if it was here and now. I'm trying to make sense of hundreds of Mia's poems, in countless documents, with nothing dated or any rhyme or reason. It will be a fucking miracle if we ever finish this. To a standard that we are happy with, anyway.

Control

By Miya Squirrel

She remembered
We aren't
In control
Cherry was here
She

Couldn't stay
Had to be inside
Working hard
With
The others

There are more to come
But it will be easier
So much work
Has been done
Inside
And
Out

We
Be
We
Wait to see
What happens next

Berlou came back, that's what happened next. In this book, anyway.

> "Hello it's Berlou. Basically all our fusions have come undone. Oh the only two left are Mia and Jessica and me and Alex, but they had nothing to do with the mass fusion of last week. As Caris said when she came back it's not a failure - we've all grown and learned a lot. Oh wow, we actually walked in someone else's shoes, albeit someone else in the same body?! Haha. I imagine it must be hard to grasp for non multiples (normals seemed wrong haha) that we really don't know a lot about what each other are feeling. Now I've lived as Amber (and hearing Mia say there's a poem there is still annoying) it's different. Stef came back this morning/early aft. In the bath. Just suddenly realised she was Stef lol and yay amnesia means it's like 'ok wtf just happened, let's examine the evidence'. Miya then had the realisation that they were happier separate

too, so poof they undid! Poor Amber lol. She's resting. Oh age, um I guess early 30s. Late 20s. Who knows. I'm ageless unless I'm seven like Mia - Berlou."

Alone

By Mia

Finally alone
Jessica left me
Said she's taught me all she can
So I'm alone now
Just Mia
Yay!
It's been a while
But now
I can be myselfs

So, yeah. They were all 'coming undone' and I had left Mia. We now had two writers. And someone who could narrate.

Maya

"Maya's back to awful. Hoping she improves soon. My book is now about 100 poems! Jessica's started going through it and is narrating to explain the nonsense! And we have a tonne of pretty words in the children's book that got abandoned so my book is about to get proper good! Jason is a good boy! There's snow! Berwoo just rocked up. She likes writing poetry too so we're gonna do one each! Hers are 100% better than all mine put together, this is her latest. She's obv a genius. I'm taking credit. - Mia."

My poems

By Berwoo

I don't think
My poems r
Very gud
But sometimes I
Like to do them
So I do

Mia mentioned that Maya was back to being an anxious wreck, it was rough, again. Mia made questionable art with it.

Thanks Maya

By Mia

That moment
When you think
Of stepping
Into traffic

Thanks Maya

Alone
All day
No one
To talk to

Thanks Maya

Yay
Lying in bed
Doing nothing

Thanks Maya

Unbearable
Anxiety

Thanks Maya

You think
I'm being cruel
But she's laughing

Thanks Maya

Being no one

By Maya

Mia or Miya
Wrote a poem
They said
I could be no one
I can
It doesn't always work
But
You learn
How to be small
Avoid eye contact
Your body language
You can shrink
Into yourself
You speak
Only when you have to
Using as few a words
As you can
Quietly
But loud enough
So they hear
So you don't
Have to repeat yourself
You never admit anything
You don't know
Never have
Maybe they'll take pity
Maybe they'll leave you alone
Today

And Berwoo was still writing too...

A thought process poem

By Berwoo

I was pondering a poem
Maybe either

My name
Is Berwoo
Because
I'm Berlou
But I've got
Woo

Or would

My name
Is Berwoo
Because
I'm Berlou
But I've
Got woo

Be better

Then someone said

And not
Poo

So I guess it's

My name
Is Berwoo
Because
I'm Berlou
But I've got
Woo
And not
Poo

Maya was processing through poetry, she'd just been writing for days as Miya...

Being Miya

By Maya

It was ok being Miya
I was around more
But I lost myself
We probably
Just want to be
Functionally multiple
I'm not always happy
I carry doubt and insecurities
But I like being me

Told you they wrote.

Ray of Sunshine

Disappointment

By Maya

I thought I'd left
A lot of
My anxiety
My self destructive tendencies
My pain
Behind
I hadn't
I still have work to do
I'm sorry

Maya was about to find someone new, while writing, who would make things at first a lot worse, but then much better, as per every other trauma holder.

Finding Ray

By Maya and Ray of Sunshine

So much
Anxiety
Coursing through
My veins
I don't
Even know why

It's so intense
I ask
It says I'm sad
I say
Why
It says
I want to be loved
Why don't you like me
What did I do to you
I say
What do you mean
It says
I mean
I need
You
To
Love
Me
I say
But how can I love you
When you hurt so much
It says
I just need a cuddle
I give it a cuddle
We cry together
It says
It's protecting me
To keep me safe
I'm delicate
I get hurt
If it hurts me
No one else can
I say

Oh
So you're a persecutor
Like Kai
I remember
How we healed Kai
But can my anxiety
Be healed like that
It belongs to me
It's part of me
Stop calling me it!
I'm me
I'm here
I'm valid
Mia!
Ok ok
Hi
Do you have a name?
Um
Nope
How old are you
I go
Ok
Love you

We chatted to her, got her on the phone to Granma, she cried that she missed her Nana, we knew no one had properly cried about Nana, and should have seen it coming. All her memories were of their living room in the big house, playing with Barbies, with cuddles and reading The Famous Five together - "You're taking liberties, my girl", when it was bedtime, but we wanted one more chapter. Putting far too much sugar in a cup of tea, and then enjoying the sugar lumped in the bottom of the cup! (Amber said, "It's no wonder we had so many tooth fillings!" And we made that exact drink for her - it was horrible!) And she soon picked a name, and poemed about it.

Me

By Ray of Sunshine

My name is Ray of Sunshine
I chose Ray
After a sad angry dog we loved
He sad and moody and hurts like me
But Mia says my name
Is Ray of Sunshine
It makes no sense
Bc I am miserable
I don't want to
I don't want to eat
I don't want friends
I don't want you to try to make me feel better
I don't want to do anything
Forever
Until I die
Ray never felt better
He was sad forever
Mia says she will help me
And with time
I might not feel so bad

There was a minute of buoyancy, when she saw all the toys. A minute.

"Omg! We got toys! I allowed to play! We get more toys nex week from auntie dickie she giff us sylvanian family grand hotel!!!

Mia said I haff to start finding things I like she say it will help me feel better. She let me lie in bed all day but now we get up and go outside. Then she gon show me how play animal crossing my name is Ray of Sunshine which is funny bc I'm not happy I am related to Maya somehow and am little and I gots a lot anxiety. Mia says she can help me get better fast and I won't feel so bad forever and then Maya will feel better too and our arms won't hurt from anxiety. I start making a list of things I like this it so far:

Sweeties
Jason
The nice picturs on the wall

Maya found me last night when she was writing a poem about her anxiety. She kept calling me it and I got angry. I choose the name Ray bc I remember that dog Ray and he was nice but moody and sad I get that then Mia said my name is Ray of Sunshine. Sorry this is a long post I started writing and they said it ok say what u want.

From Ray of Sunshine"

It didn't last.

Snowflakes

By Maya

Bouncing around
The emotions
Won't stay still
Like snowflakes
Blowing in a storm
Trying to settle

Bed

By Mia

Days
In bed
Will we
Ever get
Out
It's so hard
So uncomfortable
When it's like this
Want to do
But can't start
Thoughts
Incoherent
I
Stay
In
Bed

It was rough. They wrote.

> "Ray of Sunshine is disabling us. She doesn't want to do anything. Barely ate yesterday. She's just swaying between full blown tears and temper tantrum noes.
>
> Amber is exhausted. I'm trying. Maya's back to feeling her own rubbish and being with Ray of Sunshine but whatever we say to Ray it's not right.
>
> Obv pouring it into writing but I think we need help please. I have a croissant and coffee downstairs but am back in bed crying. Ok I'll let her cry I guess. Mia"

And wrote.

What to do

By Mia and Maya

What do you do
When you know
Your behaviour
Is being dictated
By unnecessary
Trauma responses
How do you fight it
Entwined together
It's consuming
And confusing
You believe it's true
Because it is you
Comes from inside
Trauma is recorded
Remembered
Cellularly based
A biological
Evolutionary bonus
To keep us safe
Or Miserable

Her name

By Maya

Her name
Might as well be
I don't want to
What can you say

To someone
Who just hurts
You'd think
We'd know by now
You'd think I'd know
How to help
But in her pain I just
See my pain
I can't help

Living

By Maya and Ray of Sunshine

Living is pain
So why bother
Sugar coating it
You can look for the rainbows
But
It will always be raining
You'll always be wet
Cold
Alone
Tragic
Why bother
She says
I don't want to
I don't want it
She burns fiery icicles
Simmering anger?
What do you want
Love
She says
Just love

Travelling

By Mia

Travelling forwards
No choice
Lie and wait
Time passes
Slowly
Too fast
Wanting the future
Rewrite the past
Feel the weight slow
Ask it to share
Watch while it ponders
Can it be done?
Would it be worth it?
What am I worth?
It falters
It feels it's feet
The future is unknown
Scary
The past
It hurts
But known
Pain is comforting
For those
Scared
Scarred
Sacred
Autocorrect helps
Illuminate the path
Find
The

Words
Share the feeling
Giving a voice
To the weight
I close my eyes
I hope for
Sleep

Nana

By Ray of Sunshine and Jessica

I miss her so much
She made me feel
Special and safe
I was the only person in her world
She was the only people in my world
I love her like
She cuddled
And read to me
Yesterday
But really
It was nearly forty years ago
And she's been dead
For nearly twenty years
I don't know
What to do with my feelings
They say feel them
But I don't want to

There were lots of bad days. Another friend we haven't yet mentioned is LA. Little A is a little in another system, she and Lolly become friends in a Facebook group - Big A and Amber spoke, sounded each other out, decided they were each safe enough to allow their head children to chat and play. One evening, both systems were deep in TP. And their children were driving. I've just looked back at the conversation between Ray and LA, so sweet, pure, painful.

They discussed their feelings, with empathy and support in abundance - "It helps not to be alone with scary feelings", "I happy u our frend", "We really glad you here with us". They discuss what they know about TP, "I feel it in my tummy and my arms", "It funny coz I feeling fear in my tummy and arms hurting too", "Maybe focusing on you actually helping to calm us down", "Mummy says we trauma sharing we got to feel it", "We trying to breathe and let tears out, so much fear and so much pain", "Ur safe. Nothing to be scared of now". Last quote: "I was just resting with tears".

This support, from about three thousand miles away, I can't find the words. We're just so grateful. They were one of the first people we asked to look at our book, and this feedback, obviously, had Mia and Berlou in tears...

> "I think reading your book is healing for me. I just read a part that made me cry and cry but it feels like healing tears and it's comforting somehow. It creates a connection within the pain and helps me see things in myself. Thank you. We love you."

The TP, and writing, continued. Eventually...

> "We've made progress! Managed to wash some dishes, we've eaten more than we have been, and now she's asked to play with Lego! Only took days and days not getting out of bed and about a billion "I don't want to's" but phew I think we're over the worst of this one! Ray of Sunshine, get shining! Next! From Mia!"

Funny

By Ray of Sunshine

Mia says I'm funny though
And that's
More important than being happy
So that's alright then

Yeah, Mia's not always right. But RoS apparently thinks she's quite wonderful. Caris is glaring at me.

Simultaneously

By Ray of Sunshine and Mia

It's weird
I simultaneously feel like
I've been here forever
And
Just a few days
And I'm both like 6
And 38
And can use the word simultaneously
But fink like dis

A Real Child

Ray of Sunshine was improving. They remembered, again, that Mia + Maya = Penelope, and Mia made an interesting observation...

> "And Amber always going on about how Penelope is bipolar, it could be or cyclothymia or she's just extreme. We've seen us be absolutely disabled by Ray of Sunshine while I'm simultaneously taking over the world, one word at a time (there's a poem there).
>
> From our experiences with being fused, me and Maya don't cope well. So it's no wonder Penelope has struggled forever. So it looks like we're here to stay. Amber says it's easier to manage with us separately and Maya and RoS are still healing. Ray is making progress though, and a Sylvanian Family grand hotel definitely helped!!"

Because of how this works (not that we understand any of it), RoS's processing will have been directly healing Penelope, Mia and Maya - they're all versions of the same identity, and healing one affects them all, and the greater system, of course.

Yep, so this Grand Hotel. It belonged to Vikki, a friend of Amber's, her niece no longer played with it and Vikki asked if we would like it, obviously "no, thank you, we don't have space" wasn't an option. They went to pick it up, the niece, a real live seven year old child was there, and Vikki had told her about the children in Amber's head, and Mia was told she could be herself...

“Something happened that I didn’t expect and omg I don’t really belief it.

Auntie Vikdik had a sylvanian families grand hotel that her niece didn’t want and she asked Amber if we would like it so we went last night to pick it up (only over two hours in the car and just made it to therapy on time, and very little sleep oops). Anyway, auntie dikdongle had told C all about us and when we got there we were allowed to be ourselfs! Berwoo came out and then RoS and had a cuddle bc she misses her nana. RoS got to pick a family we could have and we got squirrels and raccoons!

I chatted to C a bit, she’s nearly 8 so I told her she’s past it, might as well giff up now it’s all down hill!! The most exciting bit is that C SAW ME AS BEING A REAL CHILD AND SAYS IM HER FRIEND!! I no belief it. I always said real life children are horrible and maybe that’s bc I thought they’d never see me as being an actual child. She wants us to go play games after Christmas!!!

I basically been crying hours bc this. I no belief it.”

I’m guessing you’ve figured out Mia can be a bit emotional. It was huge. She cried so hard. Looking back on the emotions, it’s extraordinary. Amber was watching it unfold, amazed at what was pouring out of her, reflecting on the feelings over previous years that she had been leading somewhere, there was a reason to keep going, one day, life would make sense.

The books

They wrote, wrote, and wrote. The people that had been finding Amber for MFR treatments stopped. No emails. No friends. Nothing. They just wrote (and went to yoga, and walked Jason, and tried to eat enough).

Granma remembered her cousin's son's wife had studied creative writing, had published a book of poetry and was a proofreader. Mia messaged her asking for help, Mia messaged a lot of people asking for help, actually. The poetry collection kept growing, and it rapidly went from being the original manuscript of fifty something poems, to twice the size.

They heard back from one of the few agents they'd sent the original DID we write poetry manuscript to, who said no because they published children's fiction - but that she had enjoyed reading them. She'd bothered to read them! Obviously Mia's initial response was 'this is terrible, the actual end of the world, we should just quit now', but once Amber pointed out the positives in the email, she cheered up, and was ridiculously enthusiastic about it.

Now that Ray of Sunshine had got through the worst of her processing, she was brave enough to start interacting with the few people they came into contact with.

> "We went shopping and Ray of Sunshine said hi to Zoe, a bit scowly but did lol, then Amber let her choose a soap which she was excited about and when we went to pay she's like "I do it", fortunately it was Zoe on the till so she could! We were very weird! Then she asked to go in the

charity shop! And ofc we came home wiff something for her and something for Jason!"

Yep, the old magic something-that-belonged-to-her-trick, Twinkle Toes settled in nicely with Mr Sprinkle and the other soft toys. For the absolute bargain of two British pounds.

Ray wasn't the only one making progress and plans, although she was a driver of some of it. Taking the initiative to plan the day, asking others what they wanted to do. Berlou had been wanting to make a video about switching, that got noted, and later that day she came out and did it. Amber shared.

"It's hard for me but I have to acknowledge how amazing our alters have been. We've been through absolute hell this last year, processing 36 years of unresolved trauma was never going to be easy. (Especially doing it alone - we have a therapist but it's not the specialist psychotherapy we need - Caris). Yeah ok.

I don't know if we're "getting there" or not. We get hopeful, then something or someone else happens. It's just relentless. But every healing crisis is progress.

Berlou (trauma holder #1) managed to think herself out to make this video yesterday, she posted it, was going to delete it and Mia was like hold on… it's so good, so informative, cute and funny. And I'm kind of used to seeing my face not being my face now so I'm sharing, I'm so proud.

And Mia and Jessica are blasting through their book, it's a collection of 110 poems (atm, she never stops writing) mostly by Mia but everyone I think, and Jessica is now narrating it and intertwining their children's book she started a while back.

Neither of them can believe I'm doing this. I am going to start being more open from here about their achievements. Might start posting some of Mia's poems, they're unique and unorthodox but lovely (I no belief it!) Maybe lol."

Ray of Sunshine still had some tears to cry though.

"I been feeling horrible, Amber say I'm processing it get better soon but feel so bad! We went to yoga and I cried after and keep crying and Amber says it ok jus cry so I do and i guess then I gets better but then it gets bad again!

Mia making us listen to her music and she making cookies which I excited to eat. Mia still in shock at Amber sharing Berlou's video! She all like "was that really a good idea?" Now even tho she happy Amber saying we r here.

Hope I feel better tomorrow we got massage swap in the morning then I bet we feel rubbish again. I want to do the fun things! Mia not even done a single post today! I get better. From Ray of Sunshine."

Ah, Mia's contrariness... So when Amber shared, it didn't get many likes, or comments. She knew this would happen, she was putting themselves out there in a way they hadn't before. She'd been open about what was happening since the big coming out post - but in spite of Mia's ever growing social medias they'd managed to keep Amber and the alters kinda separate, they thought, maybe, maybe not. Anyway, here she was, showing the (small - ok, a few hundred people) world of her own Facebook account Berlou and Mia, chatting about switching. Saying "that is my face, but it isn't me".

Mia wasn't happy. If the post had got 50 likes and comments, she would have been bouncing. But, as it was, she felt vulnerable again. People were looking at her, but it wasn't on her terms. I think she will always struggle with 'look at me, see me, validate me!' And 'stop looking at me ur just looking because you think I'm weird'. Yeah, she knows, she says she'll figure it out.

And, as Amber mentioned, I had started intertwining the children's book, assessing the status of the statuses, and seeing what the hell we have here, if anything.

> "Help! I've unleashed a monster! Jessica won't stop writing. I like the obsessive behaviour when it's me obsessing, but it's boring watching someone else work! Hmmph. Occasionally there will be a bit of poeming to do but mostly she just narrating and intertwining all this chaos (oh yeah, u were sick of reading my nonsense months ago but I win!) into the poems and other writings."
>
> She says I'm lucky she's stopped and I can take Jason for a rainy walk! She is mean! It's still my book. My name first. MIA and Jessica. Oh shut up whoever said what about Amber? She done nowt but unknowingly drag our sorry selves around for 4 decades - if u don't no who I am pls unfriend me now."

I'd unfriend her, tbh. I'd realised we had a complete account of what happened this last year, it was patchy though, where was Kai? What happened in the beginning? I found my answers, Mia found my answers. Trawling through the notes app, she found poems, conversations, meetings, all sorts, of 'gold'. When we realised we would have to write prison, someone remembered Isabel already had - alright it's a police complaint, but it's another tone, another perspective, another glimpse into this chaos. I remembered the few blog posts Amber has written over the years, there may be clues there. It was becoming a big thing. Intricately connected to our own healing. Seeing the last year, in black and white, growing in pages every day (not fast enough for Mia though.)

Writing

By Mia

We write
Copy
Paste

Write
Delete
Tweak
Copy
Paste
Where was that?
Write
When was that?
Copy
Copy
I lost my clipboard
Previous version
Copy
Paste, this time
Copy
Paste
Delete
Write
For
Ever

Mia was busy working on her Instagram fame, one hundred followers and she's telling people "I'm basically Instagram famous now". I honestly think she understands that she isn't, at this point she just enjoys being absurd.

Others were, occasionally, allowed to write, too. When Mia wasn't sitting in the back shouting "type faster!" (I'm not sure who it's against, but I think she thinks we're in a race with someone, she says I should stop talking nonsense and type. I am typing. Not this. I'm going to bed. It's 8am, I've been collating and narrating for hours, again, after not much sleep. I'll be glad when we are done.)

Happy

By Ray of Sunshine

I just sitting
I play my game
I ok
Kinda
Happy
Say
'Is this ok?'
She says
'Yes. You enjoy being alive'
I make a little writing about it
Because it makes me
Happy
To be here
I'm also
Happy
We're writing this book
I fink
It's good for us
And
It might
Be good for others too
That makes me
Happy
I'm excited
For when we feel better
We will play
And do lots of things
And Amber will work
And we will be
Happy

Maya entered a writing prompt comp on Instagram, and was one of four winners for the poem 'Chandelier'. Mia banged on about it for days. It's relevant, you're getting it again. We are making something beautiful with the pieces.

Chandelier

by Maya

She imagined
The anxiety
The past
The pain
Smashing to the ground
Breaking into a thousand pieces
Like an antique chandelier
Unbearable
But
She made something beautiful
With the pieces

And... You'll never guess who turned up, again. Often in the morning, we are blurry, we don't really know who's around. It can be pretty confusing and it's better to just get on with things and soon enough we'll know what's going on, maybe. There is currently no space in this head for anything else, all we see and hear is ourselves and this book. Narrative is constantly being examined even without a phone or a computer in front of us.

Someone had just been looking at the "Jessica realised she was narrating herself" part, in the head. Running through it, and the thoughts go... "Will Penelope leave this in? Probably". Penelope suddenly realises she was Penelope, but she was also Jessica, wtaf was going on?! Everyone else is like "Oh, ffs, obviously you're back", Mia's not happy because of M+M=P and she "always gets confused and starts ageing around Penelope!" This explains the confusion while we were writing that part too, I could speak in the third person about myself because I was Penelope too!

Mia did some pondering, concluding the only explanation is Penelope and I are the same as Mia and her subsystem - we're independent, but can blend, and Penelope becomes Jessica. Kinda a temporary fusion (we like those don't we). It was deduced that Jessica, I, am Penelope's alter. This also explained why that weird bit of writing happened in the first place, we were blended but didn't know.

So that confused me even more about the book. I'm Penelope - brilliant but bonkers. Surely I'll mess this up. Overthink. It was messing with Mia too - when we're close we can blend very easily, she can feel older and confused, neither of us know who we are. When I was hiding behind Jessica though she didn't have this problem!

And now what about my ability to write in the third person and have any consistency, if there ever had been any, was that ruined, too? Mia ran me a bath. Filled it with rocks and smells and salts. Put on Cindy Lauper - True Colors. I'm joking, she didn't put it on, but it did come on and she made me listen to it. Chastising me for writing while Cindy wailed.

Mia and I (Penelope) are the most impatient people (person). I want it all, I want it now. I want to be able to do this book in a couple of hours and it's not going to work like that. I need help. Organisation. I need patience.

Penelope was getting exhausted. Mia was piling the pressure on and the old manic tendencies were taking their toll. They'd just found several months worth of journal entries from before Isabel, et al. were freed to Facebook. So much had been forgotten. So much was important. It was extraordinary what they'd done over the last year. Constantly writing, everywhere and anywhere, with no direction or purpose other than to tap tap the feelings away. Except Mia. She knew. She had plans: "Status it, we need a log for the book. No, we don't care that it's massively oversharing."

Penigma lay in the bath pondering. She'd recruited the littles to transcribe the journal, she could have a partial break, sit in the back and half pay attention to what they're doing. They're not stupid though, have access to all the current thoughts about the book, she could pretty much leave them to it. Then that would need converting to narration/poem, hopefully most of it would be nonsense and unneeded for the story.

*If you notice inconsistencies in our story, who we think people are, when they were made, connections between alters, etc., you're probably right. Everything is guess work. Thinking we're thinking the right things, thinking we've been given accurate information from someone inside - it might have just been some joker who found their way to the front, we could have *whispers* made it up. We don't know anything. Except what we know. And we might be wrong about that. Direct any questions to Mia, we might have clarity by the time this gets off our computer. This seems like a good spot for Miya's poem 'Chameleon'.*

Chameleon

By Miya

I can be
Many people
I can
Speak many ways
Hewwo, it Miya
Oh,
Hello
So nice to meet you
Alright
Motherf*ckers
My age

I can change
It's my superpower
And that just me
I gots
Anuffer load off people I can be
In my head
But wiff them
I leaf
I go
We
Switch

So, Pen's back. There are now three of us working on the book. Mia is in charge of poems "it's my book! Mine first! My name first! MIA". Yeah, yeah, calm down, your name is first. I'm Jessica, narrating. And Pen is now feeling like it's her project too.

"We just going crazy wiff the book over here. Mostly me, Jessica and Penelope (she's back again, we call her Penigma now, was hiding behind Jessica. She's honestly more annoying than me.) There's three versions of the same person working on the book it's silly. ANYWAY.

We been going through my 80,000 status updates and we found a synopsis for the big book! Sasha and the teens wrote it months ago! One job done haha!

'... woman who struggles with mental health problems for almost 40 years finds out they aren't actually her problems and it's all the other people unwittingly sharing a brain with her that made her feel shit most of the time, finds them and makes them feel their feelings so she can feel better.'

Book status report would be its epic but keeps growing. Currently 160 pages. Still a few months of this year to fill in and got half a journal of gold from before we made the Facebook. So I'm here forever. Amber says she's glad someone else is doing something and seemingly enjoying the break. Everything else is basically being ignored. I wanna put my Christmas tree up. Hope everyone is ok. I miss people. Lol. From Mia, and Pen, hi again."

They did put the Christmas tree up. And had 'breaks' from collating/narrating by doing fun things, like writing on the phone instead. And sleep was still something other people did. And Penelope and myself, wrote this at some point. I managed to write this section three times, three different ways, I've no idea how (it's the amnesia Jess - Mia).

"One of the most enigmatic alters is Penelope, and we realised this morning that she is hiding behind me, Jessica; it honestly feels like I'm an alter ego, not an alter. We didn't realise I was Penelope until I was mulling over that silly "will Jessica leave this in? Probably" dialogue, and I said "will Penelope leave this in?" And shocked myself, and everyone else. I'm often found hiding in plain sight and the hilarious thing is recently Jessica and Mia were hypothesising that they're horcruxes, and I can't exist while they do! So I guess Jessica is my pen name, Pen name? Someone says stop."

Yeah, I read it. If you have any idea what's going on, you're doing better than me. Ah, Penelope wrote that while we were blended, ok I see. Jesus. Pen name... to quote Caris, dickhead. And horcruxes, Mia enjoys drawing parallels between DID and the HP universe, there are a lot, you'd be surprised. Maybe Berwoo could write a book about it? (Someone is shouting "don't give her ideas!!")

What was I thinking

By Jessica

Literally just forgot
What I just said I had to remember
And after a lot of effort
Remembered it was a poem called

Sleep

By Mia

We try to sleep
But
It just
Doesn't work
I think
It's a myth
The nights
Are so long

Night and day

By Mia

We're drowning in words
At night
The words keep whirling
Maybe
If I let some out
They'll calm
But
Come day
We can't remember

Even chatting with their system friends wasn't happening. Trying to arrange a time to catch up...

Amber: Yeah tomorrow, home alone all day
Big A: Alone is a relative word I think, but I get what you mean

Amber: There are children making apparently 'creepy ghost noises' behind me

I had to include it, RoS and Berwoo and the others are being so patient with us! There will be MEGA playing this Christmas. (Granma's gone crazy, toys galore, Amber's getting more spoilt this year as a thirty nine year old than she has for decades! She says, "yeah, no, I'm not, I wasn't even allowed to choose the leggings Mia decided I wanted for my birthday").

And some old faces made a welcome return, after being missing for well over a month. Lolly realised she was Lolly, and Jasmine, and Sophie, all together! Feeling good! Clearly they'd been working hard inside too.

Outside of my head

By Mia

Whoa
Don't tell anyone
But I think there's a world
Outside of
My own
Head

Nah

And more returned…

"I'm Sasha, Jas, Lola, and Soph. We're all together now, like Lolly, et al. But Peach is still separate. For whatever reason. God knows what we'll be called. I wanna be Sasha, the rest of me says no. We've pondered Kali again. Not sure. Might figure something out sometime. Lolly's just being Lolly atm but isn't comfortable and they might need to rename too."

Jessica looked at the four/one girl/s. Amazed at what she was seeing. They'd been inside for over a month with next to no contact. The couple of times they'd seen or heard from any of them they'd clearly been deep in TP. They sat and reflected on how different they were feeling. Only slightly annoyed by Jessica popping out to write. Amber was thinking, too.

Behaviour

By Amber and Mia

This behaviour is entirely normal
Just the project isn't normally this big
It's previously been
A two thousand word essay
That's due the next morning
And it's 7.30pm
So, I'd best get some beers

Throughout the whole year, they'd been engaging with other systems within Facebook groups, this feedback while offering advice and personal experiences, even affected Stef:

> "Every interaction I've ever had with your system has been so beautiful, gentle, helpful, and empathic, and I want to say a huge thank you."

I'm just, ya know, collating and narrating. Mia's still producing words.

The words

By Mia

I can't believe
They still keep coming
Amber always said
She'd love to write

She just
Didn't know what
To write about
Ta da!

No-one could say anything, no words were sacred, everything said and thought was fair game for the book or Instagram.

Honest to dog
Direct Amber quote
"I have no words
Miya's used up all my words
Oh ffs I've just given you another fucking Instagram post haven't I?"

One of the people missing a backstory was Abigail. She had been around since she and Anabel crawled out of the dormancy well months earlier. All they knew about her was that she liked reading. They wondered what her story might be, and one night in bed, watching events unfold from when we were eighteen - impulsively driving over two hours in the middle of night, because, of course, of a boy (he was horrid too - that was stoopid - Mia)*, just to drive back, another two hours, just to crash, rolling the car, hanging upside down on a little country road at 6am. There's never been any memory of that crash, of course someone was holding it. They actually, almost, enjoyed that trauma share. Rolling a car was comparably pleasant to the emotional agony they were used to.*

Days passed, and Jessica and Pen were still collating and narrating. They had twenty pages of 'spare poems'. They were getting book blind, the sensible thing would be to leave it alone, come back to it in January, edit again then with actual fresh eyes - but that wasn't allowed. Mia was frustrated. It was done! Except for the end - how could they finish it when the story wasn't over? Mia wanted to put it out there, start the process of their happy ever after, and hopefully help others through their own healing.

What they had achieved was amazing. They were sure. This. Was. It. The final hurdle of their healing. They'd processed so much, dragged so much out, written hundreds of thousands of heartfelt words. They achieved what might take years of therapy, pretty much alone, in a year.

Incredible

By Miya

We
R
Incredible

She
Wouldn't
Say it
Tho

They wanted to do one last edit, it was so close, they'd have to fill in whatever may or may not happen with a diagnosis, but there was nothing they could do about that now. Final edit, have Ashlie (Granma's cousin's son's wife) proofread. Some professional eyes on it before sending to agents couldn't hurt.

On their way to bed, brushing their teeth, it was insane. This healing they'd gone through, achieving so much. They stood looking at themselves in the mirror. Wait, this had to have been planned. They had always felt like whatever is happening here, there's always someone watching, trying to help, guide, they'd said time and again, it had to have been planned.

They wondered, but just how planned? What if even the incessant writing was planned, for this reason? Sitting around a conference room table, in another dimension (?) a couple of years ago, working out how to reveal and heal - maybe even benefit from it? Everything would be forgotten. They had no idea how much they'd be able to break through the barriers - it was two separate worlds - intricately connected, with the same people, existing in both, except one was here, on earth, 'reality', the physical. The other: entirely in this head. Limited communication between both. They could send people through, with agendas, messages, intentions, but the amnesia meant you get here - forget everything you arrived knowing, thrown into Amber's real life.

Almost impossible, but... Someone knew - write it all down, anywhere, it won't be for nothing. It wouldn't have been for nothing anyway, we've healed in unbelievable ways. With it all written down, we could reflect on it, see what we had achieved. Help others. Share our story. Two hundred and forty four pages. In both a year and a few weeks. We assume this was, of course, Penelope's plan, executed by Mia

And now, we wait. And write.

Motivation

By Amber

Motivation
She won't do it
If there's no reward
And
She won't do it
If she doesn't want to
When she wants to
And there's reason to
She's unstoppable

Realistic

By Mia

I don't know
How realistic it is
That I can ever be
A person
I'd like to do things
I'm writing a book
But
They'll look at me
And see Amber
And say
She is a part of Amber
And Amber says
She'll explain
I am my own person
To as many people as she needs to
As many times as she has to
I guess that's the best I'm getting

Postscript - October 2022

We waited, and wrote. Mia had her first poof day celebration - with a pink unicorn cake, and wrote over a thousand poems, some of which eventually got sorted and published as poetry books (the score at the moment is Mia: 2 - *Are my thoughts my own?* and *Woe is Mia*; Berwoo: 2 - *Parts and farts* and *Parts and farts LITTLES VERSION!!!.*)

We'd thought we were starting 2022 positively, but it wasn't to be. Berlou's trauma was yet to be healed and we were still suffering because of this. After being frontstuck for a week, suffering, Mia went to the police about the abuse in February. She visited three police stations before someone would speak to her and it was another three months of sitting on the trauma before the Crown Prosecution Service threw it out, no further action, no giving evidence, no abuser being spoken to even. We wondered if the processing of the abuse should be within this book, but it will be a standalone book of poetry and commentary - *Healing the big T.*

Healing the Big T is one of the many projects started and not finished this year. There are a few other poetry books, but the main projects are now Mia's first fiction book - *The Unicoracle* - in which she is exploring healing DID, with unicorns, magic and other dimensions, of course, and *The Big Book of DID Questions and Answers.*

We found out we'd been diagnosed with *"Mixed dissociative (conversion) disorder with traits of multiple personality disorder. ? Mixed personality disorder with traits of emotionally unstable, histrionic and anxious avoidant personality disorder"*. The report suggested we had false memory syndrome, 'projective identification' (we think this means we saw others with DID and copied them), and stated we should not be self aware, he even described how Amber became *"disinterested and started talking as Mia"* - yep, *disinterested*, not *dissociated.*

We were refused a second opinion, and had to fight hard to get one. Andy the mental health nurse advocated for us and was told that the diagnosis of mixed dissociative (conversion) disorder was enough to access specialist psychotherapy services, and we should have been happy with that. A month after complaining comprehensively about the assessment via email (honestly, another book could be written just critiquing the two assessments we've had), the manager for the Single Point of Access called and apologised predominantly for the psychiatrist being late to ring - that was all he could apologise for it seemed - and told us that they were trying to find someone who could diagnose DID. In August 2022 we had another assessment - in person, it was traumatic but nowhere near as bad as the first one and the outcome was a diagnosis of DID or P-DID (partial DID, OSDD) after Mia burst out after a couple of minutes and presented her 'evidence' - four books and this manuscript. Our GP has applied for funding from the CCG for us to access therapy through one of the few centres within the UK that treat trauma and dissociation.

Life is still a rollercoaster, and we are not 'healed'. Amber is still often absent, assumed attempting to heal us from the inside out. Healing seems to happen at varying degrees of consciousness, and for the most part we aren't consciously aware of what's happening. This year we've had countless fusions and separations/splits, all integration and healing, and all painful. Fortunately Berwoo is here a lot and is trying to motivate Mia and the others, after everything Mia went through, she's lost a lot of sparkle and ambition. When she put this book together, ten months ago, she had fantastical dreams of an agent seeing it as a unique insight into DID and healing, and would support us trying to find a publisher. Obviously no agents even responded - who would want to take on us as a client, and this isn't exactly a normal book either.

So, we're publishing. We just hope it helps someone else heal, makes someone's life a little less lonely, helps people be able to be themselves, all of them selves. We realise DID will never be 'normal', but it is not 'rare' as is often assumed, we hope that we can help to increase awareness and understanding, making the world an easier place for the people that do suffer with DID and other dissociative disorders, and those who love them.

- Pen/Maya fusion

Feelings

By Miya

Be nice
To me please
My feelings
They
Have
Feelings

Post postscript - October 2022

I'm back. Pen/Maya and Berwoo did an amazing job, formatting, editing and publishing The revelation *a few weeks ago. It led to a lot of reflection, everyone thought it was strange I hadn't rocked up when they started editing my (and Mia's) book. Berwoo did some pondering a few days ago, remembered how Mia went looking for Penelope, and tried to figure out where I was.*

She found this in the notes app, from April.

> "It's now April. April 20th 420. To be exact. Four months since we finished the book, it was amazing, agents bit our hands off, people clamoured to get to Mia before she was too great a star. Book and film deals rolled in. Ha, no, we sent this apparent POS out to about 30 agents over the next month or so and got a handful of thanks-but-no-thanks back. I'm sat on my bed, I'm Mia and Jessica at the moment, but others are behind me, the sun is shining, I had a smoke, I'm hungry.
>
> Soon we'll go through the last few months with all the writing and poems, there are hundreds, the poeming spiralled. But it's been a few months, we thought we were through it, a few pages ago, a minute in reading terms, four months in living breathing life. There was more to do, and now, we think, we are through it.
>
> We still don't have a diagnosis but have had positive news about that and will be getting another assessment sometime. We also found out what would happen if we went to the police about the abuse that happened when we were two."

That's as far as we'd got, Berwoo concluded that maybe I, Jessica, was still with Mia? Maybe that's why Mia had been miserable? Maybe we'd forgotten, like everything else? People tried to talk to me/Mia about it - I couldn't be seen, Mia was just going on and on about how rubbish everything was, all the time.

One night a few days ago, we spent most of it awake, we can't remember what happened, but there was a huge group effort to separate Mia and me, and we managed it. It took a few days before I felt like 'me' again, and I just hid, watching. When we got our first review of this book, I had things to say, came to the front, wrote thanking Andrew, started to spend some time out, in the body. Started thinking consciously.

I remembered Ashlie's comments when she proofread the book, that she didn't think it was finished, I started wondering if anything else was missing - that was needed for this story, before we move on to the next project (two more have already been started in the last few days, I have to move fast, and this is published, live, wrong!)

So, hopefully very quickly, let's just go back to last year, we're waiting and writing. Pen has crashed hard, now we'd stopped, after the weeks of mania, she was suicidal. Amber's birthday was awful, she wasn't here and Mia + were trauma processing, yet again. Another little TH had appeared, a Penelope, and Pen and Maya had fused.

> "It's Caris. Trying to be a little proactive. We seem to be making slow progress with the crazies: Loppy (a new Penelope TH) seems to be hung up on that "she knows" - she knows how bad it is, she knows Berlou is crying (she isn't anymore), she knows it can't and won't get better. So something to work with, maybe she did know, maybe all the Penelope drive and achieve while wishing they're dead is related to that? We aren't sure yet, we might get clarity."

And the next day...

"Alright I'll try to be brief. I failed, keep scrolling it's just a load of clarity that probably won't make any sense to anyone else but I'm blahing it and putting it somewhere. We got someone through last night from the other side to tell us what was going on with Pen, specifically what her relation to the early traumas was bc we thought she was a non traumatised alter created after we started building amnesiac walls/ splitting but (as per everything) we don't know. And it seems we're now disproving our own book

1. I know now why we write! It's access - we can't get clear thought processes here in the front because there's usually people blended. We can't think clearly. And we forget everything we think and most of what we say/write anyway. So it had to come out somehow and it seems this is the best way we've found, and this way we know what's happened (and have a best seller book lol - someone is like wtaf I thought it was rubbish yesterday? Yeah we're changeable).
2. When Michael (architect inside. There's so much more. That we haven't even touched on with the book even. Yeah it's not finished we know that now but it's good enough to send out) was here he got into the body and was blown away by the efficacy of the amnesia. Like he's chatting away knowing things then bang self doubt and asking if he's making it all up, crazy. Then he stepped back and started writing to us.
3. Mia came through Xmas Eve and split two days later - pushing out a lot of her anxieties and trauma, and making Maya. It seems this is similar to what happened 37 years ago, except it was Pen who experienced the first trauma. Couldn't cope, split, making Berlou, who cried inside for 36 years. Loppy (new Penelope trauma holder) has been crying that "she knows", so we think Pen knew, at least subconsciously. Loppy is like a wizened 2/3 year old, weird (yeah, a small person who knows too much).
4. So Pen's 'moods' (something that looks like bipolar) might be that she's been always doing what Mia's been doing - carrying trauma holders when they're close to the front. Trying to balance her own ambitions and whatever she has to prove to the world, with whoever is close and wanting to die. We know we split and fuse easily and assume this has always been happening.

5. We don't know where Amber fits into it. If the theory of structural dissociation whatever is correct, as we started memory blocking at 2, we can kinda assume there were more of us around then. So Amber is maybe just unfortunate enough to land the body's name and have to manage out here (without having any idea about what it is she is trying to manage!)
6. They reckon the reveal has taken over ten years of planning. We needed to know inside we would be able to do what we had to do outside.
7. It's all just a headfuck. How can someone be this complex. It's not fair. Now we've spewed the words someone wants to cry. Seems like a good plan. Cry, food, yoga, sleep or write or something.

- Mia, Ana (Pen+Maya), Amber, Caris, Berlou, everyone."

Yep, we were getting more confusion/clarity. After finally 'healing the big T', we are now 90% certain this is correct, that Pen experienced the trauma and split, and never stopped. A lot of alters seem to be related to her, and we've seen how easily those in her (our) 'family' split and fuse.

We haven't mentioned Michael before, mostly because this is the first time he's been mentioned in a Facebook post, and we just couldn't be bothered to open up that box of worms here, in 'The revelation' *(it was* 'The Healing', *last time I worked on it, Pen/Maya [Ana? I'm coming to that] renamed it, as they felt it wasn't all of the 'healing', but it is most of it). I'm not sure how long he's been around, but he's an angel, there's Gabriel too. We have very little communication with them, and the debate over whether or not he really is a fricken angel or is just in this head with the rest of us continues, answers depend on who you ask (someone said "maybe he's another damn Penelope", lol). I'm not sure what's been written, but by the sounds of this there's going to be some stuff in the notes and/or journal, and Mia is now planning another book, I have to help with, in which we're going to explore all the weird stuff that was too weird to include or try to explain in this (I think that means she's working on around 6 at the moment, but might be more).*

Quickly, Pen + Maya - Ana, we just learnt/remembered, and Pen/Maya, are both the same fusion, however Ana didn't last and both of them have been through many fusions this year, so are not the same people/person they were last year, they've been asked if they want to be Ana again and they say no, there are reasons for this, which we will probably explore in 'Healing the big T'. *There's currently a debate behind me over whether or not ANYONE would want to read more of this, but, honestly, at this point we just have to keep going. Publishing this has actually been really good for the whole system, and we need to see what we have there, in that 88 pages of poems...*

Anyway, apologies, I've missed a lot. Back to December, the next day wasn't good either:

> "All we do is write. I don't know what else to do. I think I'll call Samaritans they're nice. I don't want to talk to the one person we do bc it's not fair. It's not fair to always tell someone you don't want to be alive is it.
> It just hurts too much. I don't think we can do this. I don't think we're achieving anything. I think any idea that this could possibly end up with us being able to live a nice life is unrealistic. Someone was just writing and I don't even know why we do. What are we doing. Why doesn't amber help anymore. We're spending our days blurry. Barely even knowing who is doing the limited things we do. The only time we feel like a human being is in the yoga studio and sometimes when we walk jason. Like oh ok, do more exercise then! That works right? Yeah we're not eating enough to not be losing weight without doing any exercise so I think an exercise obsession would just kill us faster. Ok so obv someone's like there's a plan. We also have jumping. We think we could jump. Amber doesn't even have the strength to come and stop me posting this. Mia."

I haven't read through the comments, it's set to 'only me' privacy now, but looks like there was a lot of support offered.

> "It honestly like "what book?" now.

We've basically moved on. Keep writing. Jessica can carry on later.
Mostly just wishing we were dead. Doing a lot of writing that's probably just for us. Someone put bleach in the toilet and cleaned the sink, think it was a little. I have a vague recollection yesterday of maybe amber looking at the sink and thinking I wish I could clean that. And some littles shouted "we do it tomorrow" so assume that's that.
Got out of bed again. More liquid food. Made it to the sofa. Mostly Mia, maybe Caris, likely others."

Same day, oh my God, how did we actually get through any of this?

"Managed to walk, forgot to get cash for supplies then drove instead so went into a shop. I mean we have no idea who we are or what's going on and when someone asked if we were ok in the shop, our response was "dissociated"

Pretty sure this nonsense is Amber's. No idea what's going on or who is here. Now I'm writing I know Mia and Caris. We don't even know if Amber is here. No response so assume not. We maybe have a little related to Amber, she's said she's Amber a few times and it's different to being confused and thinking we are Amber. It was echoing loudly around the headspace that this is the last big trauma share but I don't believe anything my brain tells me now.

I hope Amber is ok. We were chatting before and like omg what are we gonna do? Someone was like "we could go to the police, that's something to do". Everyone was just like *lots of eyes emojis* We won't. But it was interesting thinking about it again, and how much has changed since the last time we thought about it. We're just so tired of this. Feeling like an alien. It's like we suddenly are on the wrong planet. We're so grateful for the friends that get it. Grateful for the friends that don't, but see us. So tired. Grateful for Jason. Granma. This is going a bit better than last night's attempts at gratitude lol. Thanks for reading.
Please send some kind of magic this way so we can be done with this and not have a crying first Christmas. We're trying. We are. But it's hard. And inside are laughing at me for just thinking I hope amber comes back

soon, it's been a while since that was my mantra lol. Mia and god knows who else, no one cba to think."

SAME DAY... This is what I knew was needed for this book, Amber never had any trauma processing herself throughout 2021 - just supporting others she shared a body with, and all the fusions she was subjected to, now Mia was realising what she had gone through.

"Wow u no what just hit me. Like a tonne of bricks. Years of trying to explain why she said or did something, with no understanding of why. And often incomplete memories to make sense of. Poor Amber. I hope she's ok. I send her love. Mia."

Then, finally, over a month after they had the assessment, the MH nurse gave us a copy of the report (Pen/Maya touched on this, it's all fun reading so yet again we're repeating ourself, sorry).

"We saw mh nurse. Got a copy of assessment, it's quite wonderful, we got it all!
- 'Projective identification' - we found out about DID and decided to manifest it! Fun times!
- false memory syndrome! Yeah! We made up the abuse the started the amnesia!
- no psychotic symptoms so that's a plus. Caris is here. It might get sweary
- omg "She said that she was aware of most of the personalities and lived the experience. This I considered was against the concept of dissociation as it happens on a subconscious level without the full awareness and control of the individual... unaware of each other's existence" I don't need to swear but thanks Mia. I'll just caps MAY I REFER YOU TO THE PREVIOUS 37 YEARS. Fml.
- he kept going on about DID not being in the ICD - fucking moron. According to Andy *(nurse)*, the ICD 11 is on its way on the 1st January, you'll never guess what's in it. Anyway. They're the highlights. Amber was here for a bit of it and said "I'm not sure I should keep this" about

the report (he gave us a hard copy) then she's like yeah it's fuel for Mia. Dr XXX is in her firing line, oh the poetry will be wonderful I'm sure.
Caris and Mia

Edit: "I advised her to read the relevant leaflets available from the website www.rcpsych.ac.uk especially about PTSD, cannabis, feeling stressed, overwhelmed and on the edge, eating disorder, personality disorders, self-harm, anxiety (I'M DISSOCIATING TRYING TO COPY THIS ITS SO BORING), depression, sleeping well & tiredness, etc. She did not sound too keen on this and said it sounded "boring".

When I explained my opinion and her diagnosis, she became disinterested for a while, started talking as Mia, telling me that she was Mia and then asked me "what", "what are you saying", "what did you just say". I offered to postpone our conversation if she was upset and she said that she had returned to Amber, and we could continue".

Damn it I had loads to say about that and have broken myself copying it. Mia says dissociation lol. "Boring", honestly if you've ever spoken to Mia you must know Amber could not and would not pretend that why tf would (Mia's going crazy behind me) anyone do that. It's not possible. Amber can barely even do an impression of Mia - it would be impossible to maintain. Andy wants to read the book, didn't even seem surprised somehow lol. "Boring" Mia is the best lol. And "disinterested" fs lol mr I've treated thousands of dissociation patients

Caris"

Yeah, it wasn't what anyone needed. It's now 23rd December, and we're meant to be going to Granma's for Christmas.

"We trying to pack. Berlou woke up. Made a video about book/ diagnosis. Think she just needed to talk out loud, it's on our YouTube. I'll put a link in comments.
Someone is really holding us back. We no it's not gon be easy. But someone is convinced it's not fair on mum/dad/bro to have to be around us.

There's so much sadness still. It is bad enough that one person has to spend any time with us so seems stupid to subject anyone else to us. It'll be a miracle if we get out of this house. I don't know what to do to fight it. Berlou's been trying for hours. Just so tired. Mia."

Respite

By Mia

Four fifteen am
We're here
I think
I'm not sure
Who is
Small people are
They're excited
For Christmas
It feels
Strange
I'm trying to focus
On the nicer feelings
To change the narrative
We've set the intention
We will have some respite
Allow
Some joy

They got home, Granma had been told by RoS Mia would need a unicorn cake for her poofday, she didn't disappoint!

"Dis Mia's poofday cake from Berwoo! She one year old! we r excited for tomorrow Mia got me b4 and I was a bit mad it no cissmas yet. I stay inside until presents! Granma made her cake Ray of sunshine say she want a pink unicorn cake! It so pretty!! And our frend LA made her a pictur, Mia so happy she cry! Hope effryone haffs good cissmas! We show u our toys tomorrow! Bye bye from Berwoo!!"

It was ok, there was a lot of overwhelm, emotions everywhere, I remember one point Kitty hiding behind the table, simultaneously wishing she was alone and also desperate for someone to save her. There was definitely one big incident, I can't remember exactly what happened, but Kitty melted down while eating a meal, I remember her thinking of all the things she wanted to do - smashing her face into the plate of food in front of her, throwing the lamp, tipping the sofa. - but she just beat our own head with her fists. Fortunately, by this point Granma's also a TP pro now, and just held her while she sobbed and calmed down. We had a lot of bruises on our head.

"How was everyone's Christmas? We only ruined it for everyone a little bit ok slightly more than a little bit and there was one event but it led to definite progress and right now no one is wishing we were dead so I'm calling it a win! Hope ur having a good second Boxing Day! From Mia and Loppy and Kitty say hi too!"

Right, that's it for the status updates. More stuff happened, it never stops, but that's it for The revelation. *All the poetry Mia was now writing went into the other books, everyone was working with Loppy, who still kept claiming "she knew". There's a lot of poetry and writing from this time that wasn't getting signed or shared, this poem/conversation (exactly as I found it) is definitely Loppy, and I assume Mia from the language.*

You don't know

By Loppy and Mia

You think you know
But you don't
You don't know
You can't know
You won't know

I do

But

I'm

Not

Telling

That's ok

You take ur time

I don't need time

I need to not exist

I need it to stop

What is happening that you need to stop

I can't tell you

You don't want to know

It's ok

You're safe

You can tell us

I don't want to

I can't

Ok

Can we just cuddle?

Yes

They carried on working to heal Loppy, it happened and eventually she fused with Ray of Sunshine, Kitty, and a load of other littles. I found this in the notes, the information we received from Michael when we asked. Many times we've been given information, had our limited little minds blown, and asked to not know whatever it was, just to conveniently forget it very fast.

"Hi everyone. I'm sorry it's been so hard, you know it was never going to be an easy time. We've tried to make it as smooth as possible, and the reveal has been over ten years of planning. We had to find a way. As Amber said, gather the tools. Gabriel, I and others have been working as hard as we can. Did we know? Other versions of us? Yes. Amber too? Yes. Since when? Forever. We've all known forever? Yes. Who are you? Michael's an architect- good place a coincidence. Is pen connected to the first T? Yes. How?

Michael just in the body. Felt really weird. Constricted. Not used to the physical. Remembered to look around. Remembered things from the life. Frustrated at the efficacy of the amnesia.

Alright. So everything was engineered, even things that were beyond our control? Yes. Wtaf tho. What do you want us to say, you wanted to know. So where is the other side. We told you before you can't understand. It's here. It's everywhere. It's not contained by the physical. What does pen have to do with the first trauma. She took it. The T. But she split from Berlou like Mia split from Maya

Loppy knows. How are amber and Penelope/Berlou connected? Ok how many ways are there infinite. Ok. Why can't we see anything inside. Because then you would know. We know now can we see please. We can't just turn off the amnesia and aphantasia. We're sorry. Can we fix it? Work on lucid dreaming. Where does amber fit in?"

I know, no one needs this crap, which is maybe why we so often chose to forget. We don't know if any of this is true/real or we're just making stuff up. There's no answer to the Amber question. The following two poems, one by Kitty, and one by everyone apparently, are the only poems that appears in this and another DID we write book (at the moment, anyway, I think.)

Kitty

By Kitty

Kitty
My name I choose Kitty
I'm sad too
I think I'm last
I'm so tired
I can't go on
How can we get better
I don't believe it
The weight
Mia speaks of the weight
In relation to grief
So heavy
This isn't grief
I don't think
It is grief
I'm grieving for the life we lost
I'm grieving for the life Amber tried to live
I'm grieving for the children who slept
Who are seeing the light
For the first time
In decades
I'm grieving for my innocence
I'm grieving for those who want to live
But we want to die more

Guess

By everyone

I guess
We write
We know not what
But it's clearly
How we process

So much
Has happened
These last
Fifteen months
And
Thirty nine years.

Somehow
We fragmented
So much
Kept so many
Secrets
From each other

And
One of the weirdest
Things is that
Once we've
Shared our secrets

Physically
Mentally
Emotionally

From car crashes
Rejections
Illnesses
Injuries
To
DA
SA

Every thing
That hurt
We all must feel
But then
We all
Mostly
Forget

We let
It go

So
We are a mess
And we are sorry
We are doing our healing
Here
With our words

We have to put them somewhere though
And they might
Help someone
Understand
Themselves

Or not

But
We don't know what else to do now
Our words are
At the moment
All we have

As we try to
Put ourselves
Back together

Thank you
For your
Patience

All of us

So, Amber was finally 'being processed', too. Kitty came and changed a lot for Mia, who you can see in the status update however many pages ago, suddenly realised just what Amber had gone through the whole life. There was a lot of writing this Christmas, most of it woeful and very depressing, and a lot of it became Mia's second book of poetry 'Woe is Mia', *which is also her biggest book of poetry (so far), and is 250 pages of processing depression and suicidal thoughts.*

Berlou's trauma was coming up again, each time it had been visited, it felt like huge healing had been achieved, but it was never enough. Berlou was improving, with every painful processing session, but it was still there, bubbling and festering, impacting the whole system.

We cry

By unknown

We've been
Peeling layers
For so long
We're too tired
We can't do it
I don't have the strength

The children ask
Will it always be like this?
Why do we suffer?

Someone
Usually
Has some positivity
But
We just can't
At the moment

We tell them
We are broken
Because of what a man did to us
When we were little
The letters shine they resonate tap tap this is worth it
We cry
They cry

We be together
We hope
For respite
We know

Nothing is permanent
But when
It hurts
This much
It's hard to imagine it not

A lot has changed again, these few weeks since Berwoo and Pen/Maya decided to tackle this monstrosity. The last couple of days, we've been almost manic again, Amber's present, trying to get on with her own stuff but understanding we need to do what we need to do, and is supporting us. From here, it's mostly just healing that damn big T, which we'll explore sometime, hopefully soon, so we can properly let that go once and for all, we hope. Berwoo came up with a new book title - 'yes we DID' *(all the lowercase titles, as with* The revelation, *are a stylistic choice by Mia - would you want to argue with her?)*

Mia's keen to get on with 'yes we DID' *- at first we thought maybe it could be all the weird stuff, that's too weird to go in here, but then someone pointed out there might be a worthy story around the publishing of the four poetry books this year - Mia's two will probably be touched upon in* 'Healing the big T', *but I have a feeling there's some story about Berwoo and her endeavours this year while being 'the boss', for a while, and publishing her own two books of poetry -* 'Parts and farts' *and* 'Parts and farts: LITTLES VERSION!!!' *- which is basically a whole load of full colour, highly decorated nonsense, which she and Lolly made in a couple of weeks, she's excited that I might do this - when she published* 'Parts and farts', *we weren't on social media, and while Mia often has thoughts about making videos/posts promoting Berwoo's books, space and time is hard to come by in this brain.*

I'm not sure how to end. I've not been here for months, and now I'm back, everyone is happy, we're maybe a bit manic and disorganised at times, most of the time (the laughter behind me), we might be through the worst, or we might not be. But no new alters have come out since last December, so we hope we can now move forwards, pretty much exactly two years since Isabel and Amber started communicating (Amber made the comment, 'another two years' in her foreword she wrote for Pen/Maya and Berwoo, but deleted it as there had not yet been any reference to the two years, or it's significance for us).

We'll maybe never be stable, we don't know, but we've healed the best we can, with the tools we've had. Sometime we'll probably get some specialist therapy which will be interesting. The more optimistic of us are hoping this won't be necessary, but we are, as per usual, expecting the unexpected.

I'm done, I think...

-Jessica

Glossary

Age sliding: literally that, alters aren't limited by time like in the physical world. It is usually uncontrollable by the alter and depends on their feelings or external influences.

Alter: a single person within a DID system. It comes from alternate states of consciousness (we like that one) or alternative personality (we aren't fans of the word 'personality'). Other terms used include parts, headmates, facets. May not identify with the physical body and can be a different age/gender/sexuality/species.

Co-conscious (or co-con): when several alters are in the front headspace, the consciousness, simultaneously. They can speak to each other internally and can switch more seamlessly. We're finding we function best when we are a team, often unaware of who is actually doing the external things. We think this is likely how we have always functioned, but we all thought our thoughts were Amber's.

Dissociation: feeling disconnected from yourself or the external world. For some reason writing this is making me dissociate so Google is your friend here please.

Fictive and factive: alters who are introjects from an external source. Fictives are based on fictional characters and factives are based on real people.

Fragment: an incomplete alter, may be related to a thought or action, might have one specific memory or emotion, do one specific task... We have a few, I, Jessica am one - my only interest is writing, I've no want or need to experience more of life than that.

Fronting: being in the body, controlling it, making the choices. Or just being 'out'. Co-fronting is also a thing, what we described earlier when we spoke of being co-con and not knowing who was doing the doing.

Fusing: the merging of two alters, the opposite of splitting. Can happen between any number of alters and isn't necessarily permanent. Final fusion or unification are terms used for the fusing of all system members into a single person, often not desired by systems and functional multiplicity is the aim. Again not necessarily permanent, stress or trauma can lead to splits, once the brain knows how it doesn't forget.

Gatekeeper: an alter who controls access to memories or the front.

Host: the alter that has lived most of the life, is sometimes ultimately 'in charge' of decision making.

Inner world: It's thought everyone has one to some extent (not researched, that's what our therapist said when we asked). It is where alters are when they aren't in the front, and as with everything else about these disorders, are unique to every person. They may be worlds, just a house, a void, in Miya's words... "You're only limited by your imagination", we think ours is epic from what we've seen.

Integration: the breaking down of amnesiac blocks between alters and good communication. Often confused with fusion.

Introject: an alter based on an outside source. May be family members, friends, celebrities and sadly, abusers.

Little: a young alter, under 10-12 ish.

Middle: a teenage alter.

Myofascial Release (MFR): a therapy developed by John F Barnes in which physically stored trauma can be released.

Persecutor: an alter who harms the body, system, or other alter/s. Usually with good intentions, they may be created to control the system to prevent external abuse. They can be solely internal or can be 'fronters', often responsible for self harm.

Protector: Isabel and Stef are ours. An alter whose role it is to protect the system. May be emotional, physical, sexual, and internal or external. The line between persecutor and protector can be blurry at times!

Split: creation of a new alter or fragment. May be from the host or another alter.

Subsystem: a system within the system. There are many different types and ways they may function. For instance our Mias function as one - there are many of them but they are all Mia and do not desire individual alter status or time out. Penelope also has a subsystem Mia is within, and is, we think, our most prolific alter creator.

Switch: changing alters in the body/front. May be triggered by positive or negative triggers or just because we want to.

System: the collective term for all the alters in one body.

Trauma holder (TH): an alter that holds a memory or emotions from specific trauma/s.

Trigger: something that may function as a PTSD trigger - a reminder of trauma that activates symptoms, fight/flight/freeze response, or panic. Or anything that can cause a switch, can be positive or negative.

List of Poems

Praise for 'Are my thoughts my own?'

'A courageous and powerful collection, which shines light on perhaps the most misunderstood of conditions.' - Andrew Lawes, author of Dancing With Disorder

'As a DID system myself, I relate so much to DID we write's poetry. Not only do they capture the struggles and emotions I face on my journey with DID, but they also incorporate the messages of hope and encouragement needed to press on towards healing. The messages they share with each other in their poetry are the same messages I've learned to repeat to my selves as we heal from our trauma. I recommend their poetry to anyone with DID because it reminds us that we are not alone, and our struggles are shared by others who also continue to press on towards healing.' Claire Lefferts

'I am honoured to have been given the opportunity to read this collection of work before it goes to print. This is a beautiful collection of poetry both heartwarming and heartbreaking in equal measure. The descriptive and relatable words and themes pulled a deep ping of recognition from my soul. What beauty there is to be found in such painful journeys of self-discovery. This collection is a healing balm, a reminder that sharing our stories can heal and empower those who haven't found their way through the darkness just yet. Light dispels darkness and may this beautiful system continue to let their lights shine brightly, to illuminate the truth and reality of DID with such artistry, clarity and pure honesty.' Joanne Murphy, owner of Return To Om - Womb Connection, Reiki, Yoga & Massage.

'A book of heroic and rebellious verse that offers insight into DID, voiced from the perspective of many of Amber's alters.' Alison @meh_poets

'This collection of poetry perfectly paints the abstract picture of what it's like to live with a dissociative condition. A real achievement in giving a voice to those society often does not hear.' Katja, Sorry My Mental Illness Isn't Sexy Enough For You @livesnotlabels

'Searingly honest and hopeful' Michelle Smith @snow.white_writes

'Comforting in how relatable it is. It reminds me and my system that there will be those who understand, even if there are those who judge our "failure" to lead a "normal" life. This journey is not about them. It is for each and every one of us survivors, and it's not for the faint hearted.' Jus

'As a recently discovered DID system myselves, "Are my thoughts my own" was a painfully and profoundly beautiful read. These poems have put words to experiences we thought we would never be able to explain or share with anyone outside our own mindbody. Reading this collection of poems inspired us to paint for the first time in our life; a brand new means of expressing our emotions and experience. We are forever grateful for everyone who took part in penning these words. We believe this book has the power to inspire and comfort not just other humans living as multiples, but also anyone recovering from trauma and on a journey to discover and truly believe that they were always enough.' M

'A wonderful book of poetry, giving a fascinating insight into Dissociative Identity Disorder. Not only is the reader taken on a journey through the minds of the many identities of the author, it is also a collection of beautiful poetry full of emotion. I very much recommend this book.' Pat Burton @pat.burton.poetry

'A thought-provoking poignant book of poetry which truly gives an internal perspective of this distressing complicated disorder.' sabrinas_poems

Thank you so much for reading. If you're struggling through your own healing, we know how hard it is, keep going, it's worth it. Love and patience, lots of love and patience.

We also want to share others' stories and give other people with DID a voice, we're hoping to collaborate with DID systems on anthologies that will help those writing, empowering them to share their stories, helping readers navigating their own healing journeys, raising awareness of DID and countering the immense amount of misinformation there is about a disorder caused by trauma, which is very difficult to diagnose, accept, and heal from.

If you'd like us to help you share your story, get in touch with us at did.we.write on Instagram or did.we.write@gmail.com.

Printed in Great Britain
by Amazon

33177797R00195